George William Bagby

The Letters of Mozis Addums to Billy Ivvins

George William Bagby

The Letters of Mozis Addums to Billy Ivvins

ISBN/EAN: 9783337136758

Printed in Europe, USA, Canada, Australia, Japan

Cover: Foto ©ninafisch / pixelio.de

More available books at **www.hansebooks.com**

THE
LETTERS
OF
MOZIS ADDUMS
TO
BILLY IVVINS.

RICHMOND:
WEST & JOHNSTON,
145 Main Street,
1862.

PREE-FASE.

To the Bois In the Ommy.

Deare Fellers:

Mr. Weston Jonsum have kinely printed my Letters in a Booke, fer yo bennyfit manely. I wisht it cood uv have apeared while you all wuz in winter qortuz—it mighter wiled away a tejus our or 2. But heer it is ennyhow—better late than nuvver; and here s a hoapinge it may give you a harty laff or too and drive dull keer away a short distunce. But he will come agin—keer will—fer thar is hevvy werke to be dun befo this war is endid, and the Yankis sent yelpinge back to thar ingun and codfish patchis.

Huminly speakinge, the day uv travel and trubyoulashun is apun us, and thar is no help in man,—the verry time, bois, fer Ole Marster to step in, and show what He kin doo fer a gallunt peepul, desertid by all the werld. He'll do it, too. Let's do all that a brave and detummined peepul kin doo, and, as sure as thar is pity in the Almighty heart, thar will be, in less than 2 munths frum this tiem, an exbibishun uv Divine Powur which will maik the nations trimble. Remembur Shadrack, Meshack and Ebednego in the firy furnis. Dont you know that the littil Gaim Cocke alwais whips the big Dommynicker? The big rooster sumtiems falls on the littil one and knocks him doun jes becos he's hevvy; but the littil feller rises and socks his gaffs into him, and shouts victry in a loud vois. I remembur a cais uv this kine that hapin'd at my Ant Betsis in the couny uv Cumblun, five and twente years agoe it wus, when the big Dommynicker got whipt that bad tel he went behine the ise-hous under a hunny shuck tree and hid heself for dais and dais, with the sorist hed and the wuss looking berd ginruly I uvver see. Maybe he deseastid intily, but I wont swar to that. The ise-hous ripresents the Noth, and the big Dommynicker is the Yankis. And we is the littil Gaime Chickin that dun the bizniss fer him, and remaind Cocke uv the Walke foruvver arfter. Soe stan to yo guns, trust in the Lord and keep yo powder dry.

I deddykate this Werke to the noble fellers that's a fighting for the cause of liberty, honesty and good morals, aginst the religion of cheatinge, aginst mob law, and aginst fenattycism, which is the sum and substunce uv Yanky Doodil, as he has manafestid himself to us and to the rest uv mankinc. But because he is a good fellow, and because I like him, I deddycate this po Volyum mo pticklully to one uv my carrickters, "Oans," which he is now Captin uv Cumpny "A," Levinth Rigment Ferginny Vollunteers, and, at last acounts, Actinge Inspecktur Ginrul uv the Ommy uv the Pertomuck.

Rispeckfly, dear fellers, yo obejunt servunt,

MOZIS ADDUMS.

Richmond, March 3d, 1862.

LETTERS

OF

MOZIS ADDUMS TO BILLY IVVINS.

FIRST LETTER

FROM FOMVIL TO WASHINTUN, BY WAY OF RICHMUN.

Washintun Citty, Dec. the 14, 1857.

To Mister Billy Ivvins, Kerdsvil, Buckingame Cty, Ferginny.

DEAR BILLY:—

You reclect lass summer arfter I had puffectid my skeam and had detummined to go to Washintun citty, I promist you to rite freckwently if not oftner, and to give you an acount uv all I seen and dun. Well, I've bin hear more'n a weak and has writ nar time yit, fur the reesin that I has seen so much, and has bin so bizzy I kuddint think, much mo rite. Billy this ar the dirndest place on the fase uv the erth. But I'm a going to begin at the beginin.

I took the car at Fomvil on Fridy, a onlucky day. It were the fust time uvver I took the car, but I warnt skeered, becos I had seen the car a menyer time befo. The sensashun produced upon the mine ar that uv rapid travlin, but no man, I doant keer how good a rethmetishun he is, kin count the pannils uv the fense a going along. But the mile stones aint like it twas in a grave-yard—that's a lie, and aludes to the telegraf posses. The High Bridge did'nt skeer me nuther, and I wunder it skeer ennybody, fur the injine goes over it so slow that ef the blame thing was to bust thoo, we'd all be ded befo we could pos'bly git akrost. Bimeby we reecht the Junkshin, whar I tccht about three fingers uv ball-fase whisky which I kinnot admier it. Nuvver do you mend yo drink at the Junkshin.

Leevin uv the Junkshin, my hed a buzzin with the striknine whisky, we got upun the Damvil rode, and thar the car farly ript it along, going a bumblin like litenin upon what they call the stop wrail, which ar not a sollid wrail, sich is they have on the Sowthside rode, but nuthin mo nor less than a wagun tire nailed doun to a rarfter.

I notist that the peepel in the car sot their eyes on me mighty keen, and fur a time I wus alarmd, feerin I had let loose my skeam which corntinually orkupide my mine. But it wus nuthin but the atentshun which a stranjer naterally adtracks. I shill not dwell upon the minushee uv the jerney: sufice it to say, that, twards dark, we bulged down frum the piney ole feelds and the cole pitts to the ruvver, which we skeerted with rapidity, the injine settin up a loud shout as we went howlin into the toun uv Richmun. Plegg take them bridgis! it takes no less than fo bridgis to cross the ruvver at this pint, and you ketch a site uv toun jest in time to git intoo a nuther bridge and see nuthin.

Billy, I kin not furgit the howr I enterd Richmun. Ef the fac uv bein the fust time I had paid my visit to a toun of great dimenshuns hadint bin the fac, the okashun wood still have bin momentious and foevver imprest itself upon my memry, frum this suckumstunce. I wus skeered too deth—littrilly, and no jokin, skeerd too deth!

Skeerd? Mozis Addums don't git skeerd about nuthin. But I wus tho' I sot thar trimblin and sweatin, not knowin whether to move han nor foot, wharas the rest snatched up thar little umbrellers and things and put out like a gang uv wild turkies. I didn't budge. Sertny, I felt my insignifgunce in the midst uv them thousings uv rich merchonts and edjucatid peepil, not knowin nar, single, livin 1 uv 'em. But twarnt that that skeerd me, Billy, and I warnt afeard that sumbody was goin to hert me, for I has bonier nuckles than most men and you no the size uv the frog in my arm. It were the all-fired, the owdashus, and tremenjus nois that skeer'd me. It wus enuf to uv skeered me.

May be you've heerd two injines hollerin at wunst. You've heerd the wind bellorin in the woods like a bull travlin to a cuppen thoo a bresh pile, and peepel shoutin at camp meetin and 'lectshuns, and crows holdin uv a debatin sciety in the evenin. You've hearn them things. Also you've knode the devil to git into the fowils, and the turkees git to gobblin, and the geese to cacklin, and the Ginny chickins to havin uv the hiccups all at the same time, hard as they kin stave. Well, jest imagin all them noises tangled up like a fishin line and comin right slap into yo' nakid ear when you did'nt pretend to ixpec it. Taint nuthin, taint beginnin to be nuthin cumpard with what I heerd when the car stopt in Richmun. And what you reckin this horrid rackit wus when I come to find it out? Why, it precedid frum a passel—I don't think thar wus mo'n two duzzen uv 'em, but I kuddent see strait at the time—a bout two duzzen uv the wust, the derndest, sassiest, big-mouthdist carridge drivers hollerin at the peepel to git to carry thar things, trunks and so foth, to the tavuns. Nuvver, nuvver, did I heer the beet uv it. It mighty nigh distractid me—and I has sense bin told that thar is forty odd deff peepel in Richmun and 9 in the loomatick from them very carridge drivers—but, for some reesin or ruther, I spose thar is a reesin, they calls a carridge in toun a hac. May be the carridges thar is made uv hacberry. I don't no. But them plegg-goned drivers ought to be whipt day and nite, pennytenchrid in fac.

Kunsultin the importunce uv my skeam, and havin heerd uv the place befo, I went into the crowd uv them drivers all hollerin "take yo' baggige, sir;" "carridge, sir;" "hac, sir;" "Poter fur the Sin Charles;" "Poter fur the Merrykin;" "Poter fur the Ixchain;" went right into 'em, and havin getherd my sensis, gradyully discuvvered the nigger uv the Ixchain and kollerd him.

Sais I, "I want to go right home with you."

Sais he, very plitely, "gimme yo' checx, yung marster," and I not knowin the meenin uv checx, follud whar he pintid. untwel I cum to a splendid, paintid kind uv a sirkuss waggin with a heep uv winders and reel velvet seets on the sides, and steps to git up at the hind part uv it. But the Ixchain nigger he cum right behine me, and got arfter me agin 'bout my checx. Billy, the very devil wus to play, and I mighter knowd it fur startin on Fridy. I can't take no time to tell you what checx is. Think I hadn't lef my confoundid ole trunk, mar's best har trunk, at the Junkshin? Fust I wus distrest, becos I thought I were lost, fur you know what wus in that trunk wuth munny; then I snortid and cussd mysef into vulger frackshins. In the eend I paid a telegraf to the Junkshin, and the cussid trunk come down the rode the nex mornin befo day.

The Ixchain ar a magnifecshint bildin. Thar is two uv 'em, knectid by a bridge, which spangs the street and which is better'n a house in Buckingame county. One side the street is filled with 1 hous and the other side is filled with the other hous: the bridge jines 'em, is I sed. The hous on this side has pillows higher'n a tree, and the hous on that side has, I recken, more'n a thousun winders. All Fomvil could git in that tavun, and it not feel it. Inside the hous, Billy, it jus' dazzles you right up. Marbul floes, laid in dimunds; lamps uv solid gold, hangin doun like the branchis uv a white oke, and lightid with what they call gas, a kind uv nuthin, like the ar, which smells very loud when it aint lightid, but when it is burnin, makes every thing like broad day. Then thar is lookinglassis, framed in gold, big is the side uv a con-hous, and picktchers and paintins, and a splendid bar-room and a eatin shop filled with tables, and mo niggers and people and trunks and hacs and sirkuss waggins, (which is called hominy busses,) comin and goin and talkin and smokin and drinkin and eatin and chawin tobacker and goin up stars and a comin doun and ringin uv bells, than you uvver heerd uv. I kuddent eat nothin the night I got thar, for lookin. They've got a thing thar to tell when supper is reddy which it is called a gon, a roun peece of sheet-iun a little bigger'n the hed uv a flowr barril. A nigger comes along holdin uv the dredful thing in one han' by a string uv twine, and in the other han' he's got a kunsern with a handil sumthin like the handil uv a skroo driver with the little eend uv it stuck into a trabball. He knox the gon with the trabball, and I jes' tell you it soun's mo' like the day uv jedgement wus comin than ennything I uvver heerd. When I fust heerd it, my har riz rite up like the teeth uv a wool card, and I wus a heep mo' skeered than when the carridge drivers was a hollerin so at the deep O. But seein no body didn't mine it, I nuvver let on, and you is the fust 1 I has sed a werd too about it. Don't tell enny of them boys at Kurdsvil about it. I kuddent help thinkin' what a fine thing that ar gon would be to skeer crows out uv a con-feel with.

I went to bed rite erly, fer my eyes wus a akin and my hed a sizzin. Mr. Ballud, the tavun-keeper, was mighty kine and perlite. Says he, "Mr. Addums, I am a goin to put you in a high positshun, whar you kin see everything." Says I, "I'm obleeged to you," and I follered a nigger up stars untwel we went cleen out ov site, and he put me in a long, narrer room, with a roun winder whar I could see, when day come, the tops ov a millyun uv houses with the smoke risin out uv the chimbleys and a peese uv the ruvver which rose* in the nite like a liun. The washstan uv the room was recal mogny, but it didn't have no marbul top sich as I has sense seen, the cheers wus good cheers, nuthin extry, thar war a carpit on the flo, no fire plais (but it warnt cole) and the bed mighty low doun to the groun, like a trundil bed. But the sheets was linnin and dlishus. The pillars is too big.

It took me nigh a our to git to sleap, and then I did'nt sleap but kep a wakin and a jumpin, my hart beetin, and I a thinkin about my trunk and what war in it. You kno. It come in the mornin', is I told you befo, and it wus thar, safe and soun inside the trunk. Nobody had'nt tetched it.

Billy the peepel in Richmun nuvver sleap. Oftin as I jumpt up in bed in the nite, they wus comin' and goin, travlin up and doun the passagis, treddin on the heals uv thar bootes and makin uv too much noise. The Lord only nose what they war a doin, and how they does to do without sleap beets my time. Kuntry peepel is bleest to sleap some, and me ptickly. I don't see no use uv havin uv beds ef peepel don't sleap.

Bout lite, or a little arfter, I got up, washt my fase, and eet brekfus with the passinjus goin on the car. Tried to git a tansy dram befo I eet, but they did'nt have none at the bear, fine as it wus. Ennyhow. I had a appytight, and laid in some 9 spar

* Mr. Addums means roars.

rib with aags to match,—etcetry. Smokt a fine seegare at 4punce to keep up my cackter, but had ruther uv had a pipe with some plane trash at nuthin atall.

Holdin uv my puppus in vue, I throde away about a inch and a half uv my seegare and set to bizniss. Fust I inquide fur the Guvner. They tole me, but tole me not to go thar untel 10 o'clock, and plegg take it all, I had to wait. Well, the Guvner lives in a right deasent sort uv a squar hous in one cornder uv the Captul Yard, and when I got thar at 10 o'clock he warnt thar. So I asked for ole Mr. Richy, whar he lived, and they tellin me and I folrin uv thar dreckshins got into Main street, whar thar was so menny sines and things that I got lost. Then I sees a young man, a dark complected feller he were, and had I uv them swelld faces which comes uv drinking uv whisky or havin uv the tooth-ake. I sais to him, I sais:

"Kin you tell me whar the Inquirur Offis is, whar Mr. Richy lives?"

And he lookin uv me plum in the eye, sais nuthin. Pres'ly he remarkt, he sais, very perlite, sais he:

"You see that ar tall hous over thar with the flag a flyin from the pole?" I sais, "yes." "Well," he sais, "that's the Merrikin hotell, and you jis go down the side uv it till you cum to anuther pole, somethin like that on top the hotell, only the flag aint thar, but the streaks uv the flag is ropt round the pole, painted like, That's the Inquirur Offis, certin.

I goes down and when I gits to the pole, I knox. They sais "cum in," and openin uv the winder I sees a heap uv lookin glasses, two or three likely m'latter boys, with kombs in thar har and apurns on, and a fellow standin befo a glass tyin uv sumthin round his neck.

"Ar this the Inquirur Offis?" I sais.

The m'latter boys they lafft, but the fellow at the glass sais.

"Yes, this is the Inquirur offis. What kin we do for you?" he sais.

"I want to see the editer."

"Well, he aint here."

"Whar is he?"

"He's ded and berrid—berrid bout a fornit ago."

That flustrated me a good eel, and I did'nt know what to do, but jest to be sayin sumthin. I sais:

"What did he die uv?"

"Well," he sais, "I can't say that I igzackly kno, but if you want to suscribe, I'll take yo munny jest as ef he wus livin."

I tole him, "No, I din nt rede mighty well, and hadn't no munny to spar."

With that follerd a considerbul uv talk betwixt us; he apeerin verry ankshus to fine out my bizniss, and I not lettin on. I has sense learnt that that warnt no Inquirur Offis atall, but a barber's shop. So I didn see the Guvner, nor Mr. Richy nuther.

Arfter I left the barber s shop, I reckin I went into 20 bear rooms lookin fur edters, and bein constantly fooled; fur the peepil uv Richmun has no better cents than to think it mighty funny to fool foax from the kuntry. But I did git to see sum edters, and had some chat with um, but as I was afraid to let out about my skeam, I didn t learn nuthin what I wanted.

Bein satisfide I coublnt do no bizniss, I startid roun to see the curosris. They told me Rockits were a pritty plais, and I went thar, and seen a number uv sale vessils, which is amuzin to a man what navver seen nun befo, but aint so mighty pritty ether. The merchunt s mills, in my opinvun, is the best lookin things in Richmun. By George ' they is busters. Billy, thar is mo brix in one uv them mills than in Fomvil and Ciry put together.

I heerd thar was some fine grave yards in the subbubs uv the citty, but I didn t go to nun uv um, prefearing a sircus which thar want enny in town.

The Captul buildin, whar they make the lors, aint is hansum is the Ixchain. Inside uv it thar is a likeniss in white rock uv Ginral Washintun, with a kane in his han and a plow pint, and sum mo things at his feat. I seen no ubjeckshun to this likeniss, exceptin they have drawd his stock ruther tite, givin uv a choked look to him. On the fur sid. uv the Captul I found two tremendus brass men, histed on the bottom part uv the bannisters uv the steps. One was Potrie Henry, and the uther wus Tom Jeffsun. Potrie Henry was a orrytur, and Tom Jeffsun he was the fust demmycrat, except one, which is Abryham, which didn't beeleve in no guvvermint at all, but went wharuver he dirn pleased and didn't pay no taxis.

In lookin at these gentilmen, I wus struck by the fac how much bigger peepil used to be than they is now. And I attribated the fallin off on our part to the use of bad sperrets.

Goin on a leetil further from the brass men, is what they calls the Washintun monumint, and on the rite side uv it the biggest box I uvver heerd uv, tilted up agin the monumint. Inside uv this box they tole me wus anuther likeniss uv Ginrul Washintun, straddlin uv a rarrin hoss. I reflectid apun the suckumstunce a good eel, and cum to the detummination that ef the ole Ginrul wus alive to sea the wickidniss uv these times, he'd be rarrin instid uv his hoss. But I dunno,—peepil always thinks these times is wuss'n them times.

Thar is a crowd mo uv things, Billy, to tell you uv in Richmon, but I shill not tell you uv um now. When we all gits together agin, I shill tell you. But the wust uv it all cum about by my runnin aroun to sea the things, and the fust thing I node it wer nite. I had dun miss my dinnir, which they made me pay fur it all the same as if I had eet it. This is cheetin uv the wust kine. But Mr. Ballud he didn't seem to agree with me on this pint, But he didn't make nuthin out'n me at suppur. I jest tell you I laid in a kord.

That big red-face feller which invagild me into the barbershop in the mornin, he was thar, and sot right acrost the tabil frum me. Seein uv me how I eet, he spoke up mighty peart, he sais:

"You don't seam to have no appytight."

I sais to him, "No, and ef I didn't have no mo appytight than you've got mannus, livin would be cheap whar I wus."

I sed this mighty perlite and meely-moutht, but he seain uv a kind uv a growl in my eye, shet up.

Arfter awhile I was out on the steps smoking uv a seagare, he cum at me agin. I wus lonesum and warnt sorry he cum.

"Stranjer in the city, I pesume," he sais.

I sais, "Yes."

S'e, "Buyin uv goods?"

S'I, "No."

S'e, "Leave yo fam'ly well?"
S'I, Tollibul, I thank you."
S'e, "I wuddent take you to be a marrid man, ser, you look mighty young."
S'I, "You're rite. I aint marrid yit."
Arfter that he did'nt say no mo for sum time. Peard like he wus studdyin about sumthin. Pren'ly he commenst agin, he sais:
S'e, "Goin back to Fluvanner in the mornin?"
S'I, "I thank you, ser, I don't live in no sich place as Fluvanner, and I aint a going back in the mornin. I'm a travlin."
S'e, "Fur yo helth?"
S'I, "Skeersly."
He shet up agin. Pritty soon
S'e, "Sold yo mules?"
S'I, "How in the name o' sense did you no I had enny mules?"
S'e, "Oh, we foax in town nose everything. Did you git a good prise?"
S'I, "Only far." But how he uvver come to no about them mules I sold yo par is a mistry to me. He walkt off like he wus goin away, but all uv a suddin he turned roun and sais:
S'e, "How d you like to take a littil turn this ev'nin?"
S'I, "Turn at what?"
S'e, "Tapistry, velvit."
S'I, "I don't ketch yo meenin."
S'e, "Gran plazzer, copper in the vessil, froshus animil in the jungil. You no."
S'I, "Mistur, I don't understan French, and you no it, and ef you think you're goin to redikewl me, you'll find you've got the rong sow by the year. I'm a mighty chicken-harted man. but thar is sum things I won't put up with, as you'll find out pritty durn quick ef you keep a foolin arfter me."
Then he beg'd my pardin—sed he did'nt meen to hurt my feelins, and all that. But I told him to clear out, I did'nt want no more to do with him. And I did'nt, fur you no, Billy, that when I'm mad I'm mad.
That wus the last I sean uv him, and the last advencher I had

in Richmun, from which I shuck off the dust uv my feat the following mornin. takin the North car a leetil arfter sun up.

Yo afecks nit fren, trooly,

MOZIS ADDUMS.

SECOND LETTER.

WASHINTUN. MR. ADDUMS FINDS IT DIFFICULT TO OBTAIN BORD.

DEAR BILLY:

Thar is too wais uv going from Richmun to Washintun, uv coas I took the rong way. Ef you go by one way, you kin sea Mount Vurnun in a steembote whar Ginrul Washintun were born; on the other rode, its all rode and no water. It follers that I diddent lay ize on the berth plais uv the farther uv his country, but went along all day untwell we cum to Ellicksandry, a toun that ridin a hominybust thru doant apeer to be much. Ruther dry, ruther dry, and retched to live in fer enny lenth uv tiem. But as fer bizness, I reckin its a rite peert plais, jedgin from the sale vessils in the ruvver.

To git to Ellicksandry, you got fust to git on the Centril rode and then on the Orringe rode, which it brings yew finilly to the pint; passin sum po, flat lan, and agin a trac uv tip-top rollin country, with mountings in the distans. Besides the lan and the rode running strait is a arrer—thar aint so mighty much to reckmend this wrowt, ixceptin it ar wun thing: Billy, konshent-shusly, thar kin mo pritty gearls be seen on this rode then I reckin in the hole wirld, and it bein uv a good thing to sea urn enny tiem, it ar p'tickly so in cummin to Washintun which it is the poist plais fer pritty gearls I uvver sean, and that's sayin uv a heep fer a man bawn and raist on Willisis. Thar is a appint ed time evvry day fer the car to past the deepos, and knowin uv this the gearls asembils thar in sich numbus and vriety that it acurd to me thar must be a bodin school evvry ten mile along the rode. Certny, from sum cos, thar is a cuyus kleetshin uv luvli yung wimmin at these pints.

Leevin Ellicksandry, you takes a steembote, the fust I were uvver on, havin sean one at Rockitts a good cel biggern this wun. Oneesy way uv travlin are a steembote, which it shakes with venjints in its innards all the tiem, like it had a agur, and the water belo, which, ef the consern got blode up, is boun to lroun you certin, ixceptin you wus a mity good swimmer, which I aint, being subjic to the cramps uv the laags in a ordnerry miljon. It's 7 miel to Washintun on the kontinyully tremblin steembote, but it doant look nigh so fur up the river, which it is broad here is* a hundud Appymattuxes at Fomvil, and nuthin to intrupt the vew but a few passin sale vessils.

The steembote skufflin along the buzzum uv the P'tomuck like a suaik dockter, I stud and lookt at Washintun, and lookt at it. and lookt at it. Billy, it shines in the distans uv a wintry eve- nin with a strange sort uv look. Thar it is, the grate big sitty. stretcht out upon the groun, while splended bildins and steeples and monyumints, lookin like a picktshey, which you know it is reel: and how all uv it got thar, you doant know; and who's thar, and what's goin to bekum uv you thar, you doant know: and you feal sorry fer yourself, home is so fur away, tho you left it like yistiddy. How it is with uther peepil, I cant say. but with me goin into a big sitty is atendid with a cents uv fear and danger, which is vage, and all the werse fer bein so. The housis look mitey fine, but the sky over the sitty and back uv it is dark and distrest. But the bottim part uv the sky evvrywhar is sad, evin in the mornin at sun up, ef you look at it good. I doant understand it.

Seein Washintun in the ginrul, you doant know what you sea, unless thar is sumbody thar to tell yew. I were too much ock- vupied lookin, I didn't ass no questchins. What most ingaged my atenshun was the marvel bildins, and a thing that when I cum to find it out were anuther Washintun monyumiut, the same as that in Richmun, bilt in memry uv Ginrul Washintun, only this wun is a heep higher and diffrintly shapt. A tremenjus tall, squar post of white rock, this wun is; with the frame uv a meet hous on top uv it. It sets on the ruvver bank, and a lone- somer, outlandisher thing you can't imagin. It taint finisht yit by a long shot. They tell me its to be 600 feet high, and were visin wrapidly, untwell the dern No-Nuthins got hold uv it and

* Mr. Addums frequently uses "is" in place of "as."

stopt it, sense which nobody goes anear it, and it stans thar like the pizen tree we read uv in jografy which peepil are afeard to breethe the ar in the naberhood uv it. I declar pintidly, it ar a shame fer the Amerrykin peepil to do in this way.

Next to the desertid monyumint, my mine was drawd to the Capitul—Capitul uv of the hole United States; a supup eddyfiss which I wont describe at this tiem. The reesin why I doant it aint finisht. In fac, Billy, nuthin aint finisht in this toun, ixcept it is roskallity, which it is the only thing thar is no knead uv enny futher apropriashuns fer the ixtenshin uv.

When the bote reacht the warf, (warf is sum bodes nailed down on sum stobs, stuck in the bottum uv the ruvver, runnin out from the bank, whar you stop and hitch the bote and git off at,) thar inusde anouther sean, as the Him Book says, uv kunfewshun and creecher cumplaint, with hax, and hac-drivers holrin, and hominybusses and peepil gittin off, sumthin like at the deep O in Richmun, but not so bad and terryfine to a boddy. Now I didnt know nuthin about Washintun, and did'nt know whar to go to git to stay all nite, so I stretcht my year and skun my eye, and nuvver let on but what I were intily soun on the goos, all rite, up side up, good aag.

A fello goin by sais to anuther fello, he sais;

"D'ew you reckin he'll be at Broun's?"

The uther fello sais:

"Well, I dunno; I reckin so; Broun's is a Suthun hous, you kno."

And they went on, and I went rite arfter, gittin into Broun's hominybust, fer I liked the name of Broun, it soundid so natchrul. But I didu't ixpeck thar was a man uv that commun naim in a big sitty like Washintun. It jes shows how fer from the fax uv the kais a man's idees is which spens his dais at hoam, sein only his akewaintunsis, Peepil is peepil, Billy, everywhar, and they aint much bigger nor enny better one plais than anuther; ef anything they ar wuss.

Doant you think I had unother fuss about my chex, a (cluck ar a roun, or squar, or dimunt shapt pease uv mettil, puter sumtimes, but ginnyrully brass—a brass reseat the trunk man gives you fer yo trunx when you git in the car, which you must give it back to him agin befo you kin git yo trunx,) arfter all my sufrin in Richmun? Its the trooth, Billy, ef uvver I tole it; and it cum, is I sed befo, uv startin on Fridy. I orto uv give my chex to a man on the steembote which clex um. I wont narate the bothcrashin uv it all; but it perswadid me mo and mo uv the vally uv that which were inside the trunx which give me so much trubble. I sais no mo at presint.

Way went the hominybust, goin to Broun's, hax folrin behine, and sum running ahed, grate nois irside, and the travlers sayin uv nuthin to 1 nuther, but looking out the winders to sea what they could sea. Thar is housis and peepil, uv cose, but nuthin wuth menshin untwel you git to the Smithsoniun In-titeut, which it is on yo lef han is you go to Broun's. This manshin ar not a gearl's skool, like the Buckingame Institeut, but what the meanin uv it is doant apear to be ginrilly understood. Fum awl I cood gether, the objic is to tend to the wether; you've heerd uv the cluk uv the wether; well he lives in this bildin, sumwhar; it bein vary large nobody doant verry oftin lay eyes on him. In regard uv its exturnels, the Institewt remines me uv a par uv casters. Its culler is wred, and when I has lookt at it freekwently, it looks like a hole passel uv steepills had got lost, and wus kunsultin together how to git back to the cherchis whar they belongd. But I shill hav mo to say on this pint in anuther letter. Onqueschinubbly, it are a strange kunsern.

When we got to Broun's, which we did pritty soon, I felt a fealin uv aw, fer it wer a imments struckcher. Its length, Billy, is nearly a squar, (but you doant know what a squar in a sitty is: I'll tell you sum these tiems,) and its about is high is you can fling a rock, bilt all ov white marvel the frunt uv it, the bac uv it bein commun bric, and not so high in the ar. Inside thar wus the same krowd and the same fuss that I told yon uv at the Ixchange in Richmun, only at Broun's evvryboddy was a grate man.

I liked Mr Broun. He was a small man, with sandy whiskers on his jaw, drest jam up, and verry perlite. I put my name doun on his book in my best riting with pekewlycr sattisfacshin. I follerd a Ishmun up stars loadid with my trunx, ixpectin the same granjer uv marvel I had sean on the frunt uv the hous to pervade evvrywhar. But I wus disapintid cummin to my room, and struck with recul wunder and delite. Evvrything was so intily natchrul, fer a momint I didn't know whar I wus. "Ar this a room in Broun's marvel pallis?" I ass'd myself. Whar is the fashunubble trundle-bed with the rollin foot bode, whar the marvel top washstan, the splendid bewro, the gold-embroydud kertins, and things? They warnt thar, Billy. No, thank the Lord! The bed were a good, narrer, high bed, high postid, but without any teester and vallins—jest sich a bed as the kuntry afodes most ennywhar. In like manner, the washstan uv plane wood, with a little ole pitcher and bole that lookt so frenly to me, well knowin uv thar familyur patten. The white kertin uv the winder had the ginuine Buckingame frindge, and Billy, the lookin glass were identically the same which par bought when he went to Richmun, to see Lee Fate, the French Ginrul which fot the Revolushun with Washintun. Ef thar had bin a rag carpit, split-bottum cheers, and a fier plais, instid uv a great to burn rock cole, the thing would have bin kumpleat. As it wus, it lookt so much like hoam, I laid doun and went to sleap befo I node it.

Nite had cum when I riz from my slumbus. Tryin to git to the suppur table, I got out uv doors, fer Broun's is a komplekatid hous with many passagis and star cases. The hac-drivers, standin outside with whips in thar hans, like to took me by vilents. Nuvver did I see fools mo ankshus about 1 po man they had'nt heerd uv, much mo sean, befo. They wantid to show me the fashins, but what did I keer 'bout fashins, bein uv a sighintiffick man on bisniss uv the utmus impawtents? But a carridge driver wus alwais distracktid and opinyunatid, doun to a nigger which drives a ox cart fer fodder. I cust all uv um, and went to supper up in the secund story.

Broun's dinin room aint eekul to Ballud's. Its kunsiderubly bigger, divided by foldin doughs, seperatin the ladis ectin room from the men's, and havin a vriety uv tabils. Powful ectin goes on here, speshly at dinner, which they gives you an akount uv, printid on a peese of papur, named a bill uv far. I wanted some cole chine and turnup sallet fur supper, but cudint git enny.

Uv the eetin at this tavun, which it is verry abundant day and nite, I kin dwell on it no mo, seein how long this letter drors.

Arfter supper I set in that part uv the hous in tween the frunt dough and the plais whar you sine yo name on the book, a paved plais, havin seets uv hoss-har roun the walls, and pritty orphan okupied by peepil which assembils heer to set and do nuthin. I set thar tel midnite, reading the fisonomy uv the crowd, and formin apinyuns, which I shall diliver myself uv not now. Neether ar I a goin to give you my thots uv the genrul apeerunts of Washintun as I sean it nex day in the mornin and for sevrul dais in sucksesshun. I tern to a matter uv higher impote. It ar this:

I foun that Broun charged Too Dollus and a Haf a day fur bode, with a extry charge uv Fifty Scents fer fier uv rock cole which I had when the rain cum leekin intoo my charmber. Too hocksids, and three lodes uv loose, cuddent stan this long, you may be sho: wharpun I flewde aroun to fine a wremmydy—in uther wirds, a cheeper plais, howuvver much I diddint like cheep doins in this pint uv vew, that it interfeerd with the dignitty and impawtents uv my skeam, which you understand verry well, knowing is well is I doo the vally of wrispectability in this life.

Akordingly, arfter exercizin grate jedgemint in slektin the man fur to inquier uv in the case, I (as the Bibil sais,) drawd nigh untoo a sorter yung gentilmun which set aloan frum the kumpany, whar nobody cood heer me how ignunt I wus. He wus a man of cents, evvyduntly; had him a clur, pale face, without enny beerd; and his eye wus soft and kunsiderin—not one uv them hard, sharp eyes that is alwais lookin out like a hungry shote fur shelled corn arfter it has eet it all up. His face wus cole as well as pale, and when he shakt me by the han, he barly techt it. You'll say this ar a bad sine, and I used to think so too. But I has observed this Billy:

A hickry cole has the whitist ashes, but arfter you git throo the ashes, it's the hottest kine uv a cole—and nuthin wrops itself titer roun a thing than a snaik. Tharfo I dont put no overwhelmin confidents in these heer warm felloes that shakes you so harty by the han, wroppin thar fingers tite and holdin you longer'n you wanter be hilt, and tellin you affecksnitly how glad and all they is to sea you.

Well, it turned out igzackly is I ixpected. This gentilmun, which I has sense becum well akwainted with him, arfter listining indiffrintly to my cundishin and lookin at me verry calmly took a intrust in me and helpt me cleen throo to whar I am at this momint.

His name wus Mr. Argruff, and he cums to sea me and I go to sea him. He a frenly man, certin.

Me and Mr. Argruff wus too dais goin roun to the bodin housis; I recken we went to a hundud. But he diddent goe with me to the fust one, becos I, bein like evvryboddy else, wus afeard to let out all at wunst how I wurnt abil, for the presint. too pay fur a wrispecktable plais, sich as my projick demandid. and, arfter a while, will onquestshunabbly bring. So I went by myself to a hous he pinted out to me, and when I seen the lanlady, (the desentist I has yet sean,) she curtshid perlitely, and I inquired, techin my hat, for a room. She sais :

"Ar you a member, ser?"

I reflectid a minit, and then anserd

"Yes'm, O yes'm."

She lookt at me rite good, and then she shode me a apartmint not much bigger'n a tater hole, nisely fernisht to be sho, but barly big nuff to tern roun in. I tole her I were a sizybil man, which liked elbo room. She lookt at me agin.

"Whut Stait ar you from?" she sais.

"Ole Ferginny, mum."

She lookt at me agin, harder'n evver. Then she took me to anuther cumpartmint, uv far size, but plainly fernisht as to bed. carpit, etsettry. It wer pritty dark in thar, and a few chunks uv wood, the fust I had sean, was smouldrin on the hath. She shet the dough. I felt commykill, but I sea the room was lit by a winder in the sealin, called a sky-lite. She sais, talkin rapidly, like most wimmen in ginrully do :

"This is a verry nice room, one uv the most kumfutable in the hous, and so cunveanyunt, and yit out uv the way like. Guvner Jones staid here all lass sesshin, saying it wus a charmin room; and Jedge Forney, he had it fur three years; jest arfter Ginrul Scott and the Forrin Ministers and thar ladies got rooms with me. Oh! we alwais have plesent kumpny, and my boders, bein pleesed, dont leeve me, but this is the fust uv the sesshin like, which is the reesin I have a few spar rooms, but only a verry few. The room aint cleand up this mornin, our made was taken sick lass nite, but its a fine room, the ferniteur is not igzacly new, which soots a singul gentilmun that doant like to feel crampt. Here's yo tabil, and ef you rite much, the lite falls strait down on yo papur. This winder, openin intoo the Cote." (Here she hisetid a winder, I thought warnt thar at all,) "gives you cool ar all day long, speshilly in summer. I know you'l like to set at this winder and choo tubacker, which it is the habbit with all Ferginny gentilmen, and thar is a fine wall you kin spit aginst."

Imagin, Billy, a squar inside uv a icehous, verry deep, bilt up uv brie, and a winder cut in the extreem bottom, lookin into the inside uv it, and you'l have sum idee uv this winder, and the fo walls uv a high hous runnin up around it. I sertny like to set at a up star's winder, in my cote off, uv a summur day, and spit ambeer aginst the neck uv a chimbly, but I doant admier a room with a winder openin out upon nuthin but darkniss and brix.

So we cudent agree about nether uv them rooms, altho one had a fine wall to spit aginst, and so we went up a flite uv steps to look at anuther room. You no she had verry few to spar. Well, this was a reel splendid room, but she assd too much munny fer it, and then we lookt at three or fo mo, but all wus too high prised. All the tiem I wus lookin at rooms, she wur lookin at me in a way that made me feal verry cuyus, fur I had heerd that evvrybody in Washintun, wimmen and all, wus mighty cute, and I thought I seen she knew what I cum fer. It's alwais the way with ennyboddy that's got a secrit. How cood she kno what I was arfter? The thing were ixsplained when I went to go. She diddent git mad becos I diddent bode with her, but jest as I was leavin she sais,

"Ixcuse me, ser, but didden you say you wus a member?"

When she had fust made this inquiry, I didden kno what she ment, and I didden kno now, but I wus bleest to stand up to what I had sed, so I sais agin,—

"Yes'm, Oh, yes'm."
"From Ferginny?"
"Sertny, mum."
"What deestric?"

Then it flasht upun me, and you may depen upun it, I felt like a fool. But I upt and tole her the plan fac. I tole her I had mistook her meanin intily, that I warnt no member uv Kongiss, but what I ment wus, I wus a member uv serciety.

She lafft so good nachud, I felt sorry I cudent aford to stay thar and spit on her wall. When I went back to Broun's, and had foun Mr. Argruff, (he dont bode thar,) I tole him about it. and he lafft, and sed he must go with me and help me out. So he did. We went, and we went, and went, untel we found a plais that he said wus the plais fur me, which is the plais I'm now ritinin.

Too dais we wus at it, and Billy, the Lord nose, (as your par sais,) I didden beleeve the sivvilized wirld cuntained the derty housis, and derty, po, miserbul, retchid, slip-shod, draggledy, har uncombed wimmen that I seen them too dais. Sum uv um look so pittyful, and sum so meen and feerse; and skcersly one uv um wus drest desunt. I swar I felt sorry for the sitty of Washintun; but then agin the ladies in the streat apear to have mity nisc close, and sum uv um magniffysent. How to akount fur this, I dont no. Washintun is a unakountabul plais, men is well is wimmin.

All uv um wantid me to bode at thar housis, and all offud me such indusements that I wood have takin at the droppin uv a hat, but for Mr. Argruff sayin no. One po, kine-harted cretur amost begd me to take a garrit room at her hous, reckummendin it hily

"It's a sweet, little room," she sais, "retide, and havin a good vew uv the Avnew," (that's the main streat in Washintun,) "and you wont bump yo hed in it. Thar is no fier-plais, but its rite warm ixcep in extreem cole wether, and you need'nt bump yo hed ef you be keerful to stoop. It's nicely furnisht, and the sealin slopes a leetle, but you wont bump yo hed in the middle uv the room, and you are rite tall too."

The po cretur seamed to think all wus rite ef I didden bump

my hed. I ixpec hern has been bumpt, and she is techt in the brane. Anuther reckmendid her attentive mades, anuther her nigger boy, anuther this, and anuther that. All had some grate men livin with um, and all lookt as if they sufferd much frum sumthin or nuther. I inclien too the apinyun, that many uv um drinks. They tell me the hole toun uv Washintun is a bodín hous, and that the po wimmen that keeps boders is increesin wrappidly evvry year, and with thar increese thar is a increese uv misry, you may rest ashode. In fac, a bodin hous keepin womun is a sino bode of misry, nothin mo igsept in a few kases.

When finely I got to whar I'm now, I sed to Argruff, it wer hard werk to git sootid. Yes, he said, but I had had a eesyer time and better luck than most peepil that cum to this sitty to sojern, and I reckin maybe he's rite. I stop heer, sendin my luv to all inquirin frens, and keepin in resurve a thousun things fur my necks. Good bi, Billy,

From yo faithful fren,
MOZIS ADDUMS.

THIRD LETTER.

MR. ADDUMS DESCRIBES HIS FELLO-BODERS AND SEAS AND HEERS THINGS.

DEAR BILLY:

Washintun in ginrul inside or out, ar sertny a quare toun. Out uv the hous, things is very scattrin and diffykill uv komprenshin, lookin, as it twuz, like a man had getherd together the mateyul uv a sitty, and, bein drawd off frum his bizniss, had gone sum whar to aten to anuther contrac, leevin things layin about loose, intendin to retern and jine 'um up bimeby. Its just like a feel uv wheet, which has just been sowd by a drunkin fool uv a nigger; hear the patchis is too thick, and thar, thar is skeersly a blade. The streats is predigeous brawd, givin plenty uv elbo room for everything to tun aroun, which is a good thing, thar bein so many hax and uther veekles uv all kines. The beet uv hax espeshilly, I has nuvver kunseevd. Enny man goin by 1 uv the principil tavuns, sich is Broun's, the Gnashnul, or Willuds, and seein the hax stretcht out in a string thar, wood swar his sacrid affydavid that a feunrul wus a goin to come outin thar immejitly. But they is jist waitin to take passingus, it bein sich a long wais from enny whar to enny whar. Noboddy what hassint got good kuntry laags, like mine, with plenty uv caf, and used to huntin skwerrils all day and chasin ole hars when a boy, kin stan to go from 1 plais to anuther. But I kin stan it, good, and saves a good eel uv munny tharby, nuvver takin a hac which kosts you a quartur or a haf, or imployin uv a homnybust, which only chargis 4punts.

Insied the hous, things in Washintun is jest is kramd is they is loose outsied. Eether this ar the kais, or Mr. Argruff, in slektin my bodin hous, had a cye to makin uv me a stewjint uv men and mannus. Billy, you've no idee how peepil is packt in little housis like the wun I am okkypine. Packin uv poke in a meet hous, which you shood be keerful it don't git het at the bone, and prizin uv tobarker, which y all's Winstun nose how to do it, givs you a parshil idee, but only parshil. Now in the fust plais, in this hous, which I'm a bodin in it, thar is a sto for the sellin uv men's shirts, limbur-twig appels and mint-stick kandy and doll-babis. Then thar is anuther sto uv manchermakin, wimmen's kotes and klokes and things, and that is all the reglur bizniss dun heer, at leest all I has yit found out, ixsept 1 thing which it doo puzzil me mitey ni too deth. And that ar this Lookin out uv my back winder, which ar the onliest winder I've got, thar is anuther winder jinin it to the lef, and lookin thoo that winder I seas rite into a loft, and thar I'll be konsoun if thar aint a sine bode of a tavun with a star on it, and ferther on a lite cummin in from some whar, like the lite over the top uv a fashnubble dough, and what the meenin uv it is, is mo'n I no, or kin kunjecktcher. I'v set for hows and hows, waitin for somboddy to cum into that tavun, throo that ar fer dough, and nar a sole has enturd it yit, unlest while I wuz asleap. But if enny boddy uvvur duz cum thar, I lay I ketch um.

To retern to my akount. Besides the too stos I abuv menshind, and the misteyus sine bode uv the tavun, thar is mo peepil bodin in this hous than you kin shaik a stic at, and I doant reckin I'v seen evin haf uv um eether, long as I has been heer. Uv them I seen, the fust ar, uv koas, a Kongissmun, coz evvry hous must have a Kongissmun, which genrully takes the bess room in the hons, two uv um in fac. Our Kongissmun is name Honnerbul Mister Swomplans, but whar he's frum, I has'nt a idee, only I kno he's a mitey smart man and reeds so menny books that his too rooms can't hole all uv um, so he's bleest to fill the passagis and star-casis, leevin barly room for peepil to pass. What wooddent I giv to hav his cents! I has nuvver seen him good, but he's ruther ole, and a good menny foax cums to sea him. I think they calls him Guvner; evry Kongissmun bein naterully a Guvner, a Ginrul or a Kunnel.

Arfter Guvner Swomplans, cums anuther ole man, which his name is Jedge Foskitt (evvryboddy in this toun that aint a Kongissmun and has reecht a mejum age, bein a Jedge) and he's a man of bizness in the lor, and has got him a claim agin the Govvermint, which is mostly the kais with all them in Washintun which aint got no reglur offis. Jedge Foskitt is a dredful profane man, coz I heer him cussin his washwomun, coz he can't pay her. This looks strange to me too, fur the reesin that he's got gra har and a gole heddid kane, lookin so dignyfide throo his gole specktickles, like a good ole man that blongs to the Cherch, and luvs to doo favers to peepil. But thar is wun thing about him I don't like, and that ar his nose, which the eend uv it igzackly wresembils a oke ball, sich as we boys used to make red ink out uv at ole feel skool. I kno he takes his dram freely, and its a pitty his claim agin the Guvvermint aint fur licker—he'd git it certin.

Then thar is wun mo ole man, knectid with the Post-Offis and the wrailrode. I'v heerd him torkin loud and harty freekwintly, but doant kno him when I sea him, becoz I nuvver has seen him, it bein so dark up stars heer. Livin in a leetle bit uv a room rite by this ole wrailrode man, is I doant know how menny yung Ishmen, that cums in way in the nite and gits up soon in the mornin without sayin a wird. Then agin rite over my bed is sum dutch-germuns, the saim what has the mancher-makin sto I tole you uv, and wun nite I woke up puffickly wild frum a dreem and the noise goin on abuv me; and what do you reckin it all wuz, Billy? Blamed ef too littil dutch-germun childun was'nt baun almost rite on top uv me. I jess tell you, a thing uv this sort are praps the most terryfine thing on erth. Consoun the creturs! they cries a heep, and I think a dutch-germun baby cries mo savitch than enny uther, keepin you awake, and frettin you, and disposin you agin matrymunny.

Besides all these, thar is a reel ole, ole womun that lodgis way up yonder sumwhar, and cums creepin doun stars, not makin a sound uv nois, and skeerin me evvry day like thundur. Then thar is a room for the man and his wife, which sells the shirts and candy, and thar childun, a boy bein all thar family.

But thar is mo yit. Thar is a Mr. Oans, a yung man, a Cluk (all the yung men heer is Cluks, and a good menny ole men, ixcept sich as drives hax and sells oshters), a handsum fello, with a high farrud and pritty har on his hed, which he greezis it too much, it bein the fashun in toun. He doant apeer to have no mitey good opinyun uv ennything in this werld, and goes about and looks like a man which has wrepented uv bein bawn, but, bein proud, diddent intend to apollygyze fer it. He's a genrus fello, and eets mo oshters uv a nite than enny five men in the sitty, and alwais wants me to eet with him, which I genrilly dus, not likin to hert his fealins. His room jines mine, and the verry day I got heer (Mr. Argruff tellin him I wuz frum Ferginny) he cum in and made me a presint uv a reel woodall pipe, a good wreed stem, and a hole ehanse uv splendid Linchbug tubarker to smoak. I'm bleest to like him, and sense I got to smoakin his presint, it's felt a heap mo like hoam to me. Thar is redeemin pints about Washintun.

This heer Mr. Oans has got him a fren—a little ole dried up yung man uv a spishus coprus culler, which his name is Mr. Melloo, and he rites letters fur the knewspapus, called corrispondunce, and this ar wun of the biggest biznesses in toun, ef I aint deseevd, which most likely I ar, fur the foax in Washintun ar verry fond uv lyin on all subjicks. Mr. Melloo, he rooms heer too, makin uv no fuss and behavin jist like he wuz white, but lookin pryinly at me, whenuvver he gits a chanse, pereisely like wun thease heer inkwissytiv little tan-culled beegles. I wondur ef he suspisshuns enny thing? Consoun his sole! he'd better tend too his oan bizniss and let me alone. I got nuthin to doo with him and doant want nuthin.

So you sea, Billy, this hous ar pritty well stufft with specimins uv vayus peepil. And howdyou reckin I cum to know so much about um? Why, the gearl that wates on my room, she tole me. She's white as euny lady, speeks Ishmun languidge and cums frum thar, and Billy she's plegg-taked handsum. Duz mo work, is helthier, smarter, fuller of good yumur, and better lookin than enny boddy I seen yit. She's name wuz Mayan, and I and her has a tauk evvry day. This clustraits the diffrents between Nothun and Sothun peepil, havin white mades heer, tho thar's a good chanse uv niggers too, while we all has cullud mades, likely mlatters freakwently.

Fur the ferst few dais I wer so shamed to sea this pritty gearl fixin up my bed and histin cole on my stove, I cuddint speek, and when I did speek (askin how to git in at nite, when the dough was shet on the streat) she seen frum my tremblin vois and gentmunny mannur that I thought I was talkin to a reel lady, and sense then she's got a great fantsy to me. She's got blak har, wavin, blak eyes, that is brite and quick-movin as litenin, and *smart?* I jes tell you, she's a reglar Spannish needle of a gearl. You git to foolin arfter her, like Mr. Oans and Melloo, ptickly Oans, which is alwais tryin to out do her in sayin smart things—and I be bound you think you've ketcht a razur by the blaid instid uv the handil. I think it wer Chusdy mornin I heerd Mr. Oans sayin to her—he's verry fond askin her knundrums and speakin broag like they do in her kuntry. He sais:

"Well now, Marry," he sais, "will you tell me won thing?"

"Shure," she sais, "I'm glad yure afther increesin yure infermashin. What's it, Misther Oans?"

"Well," he sais, "ken you tell me who wuz the father of Zebby dee's childer?"

"The father of Zebby dee's childer?" she sais. "Faith, I don't wonder you're askin. I think he was a ghentilmun"—meanin by this, Billy, that Mr. Oans want akwaintid with no gentilmen.

But this aint nuthen to what she sais sumtimes; I wisht I cood remember her sayins, but they is so keen you can't ketch holt uv um even with yo mine. In the weak dais, when she's cleenin up the rooms—she atends to the hole hous—uv koas she cant look verry nise, but you jes orto sea her drest up uv a Sundy. By jings! it duz me good, yes, good, to look at her. And plegg take her! she knows it. Dernd ef ole Mr. Kongissmun Swomplans doant watch her reglar throo his winder as she goes up the streat to the Kathlick Cherch. He's rite, too; Oans and Melloo duz the saim thing, and goes long to church with her sum times at nite. This 'll kinder strike you as goin too fur, but peepil duz jes is they plees in Washintun, and noboddy dont keer nuthin fur noboddy nor nuthin.

Mayan she sleeps up stars with that ar ole woman, and it ar a euyus fac, Billy, that wun uv these heer terryfine ole wimmin is kep in evvry bodin hous in Washintun. They tries to hide um, so that felloes cummin to git rooms cant sea um, but the miscrbul, po ercturs kin alwais tell when ennyboddy is a lookin aroun, and will poke thur ole skeer-faces out uv sum hole or ruther.

I'm a givin you a long akount uv all thease peepil in oddur to give you a idee uv the way things is dun heer and the kind uv foax that lives in the sitty. Now skeersly nun uv we all eets at this heer hous whar we sleap, but gits our meels at anuther hous, eunsernin which I'm a goin to tell you in my necks letter. Less change the subjiek.

When I fust got heer, Injuns was all the go—Porknees. Soos, Potty wotty mees, Socks and Focksis, and I dunno how menny mo, about 20 or 30 in number, all drest up in wred blankits, fethers, paintid faces, wrings in thar years, bar's claws, mokkysins, tommyhawks, and so forth and setry—reel Injuns, Billy. I dun seen um till I'm tide, and they doant intruss me no mo. Jeemony! how yaller and ugley they is, and how the ladies duz luv to look at um and shake thar hands! You needent tell me bout they bein Abboridgyknees, and the lost Ten Tribes uv Jeus, spoke uv in the Bibil. They is nuthin in the wirld but mlatters which run way from thar marsters a long tiem ago and dun run wild like hogs in a mounten. That's what they is, and you cant fool me, and make me bleeve yo fantsyful storis bout um. No sir ree, I used to think they wuz red like boys that's paintid thar fase with poak-berries, but they aint, they is yaller mlatters, and nuthin else.

Nex to the Injuns, it eum naehrul fur me to pay my wrispeeks to the public bildins, which thar is a grate menny uv, bilt most in ginrully uv marvel, and wood be a site to sea ef you cood eum aerost um suddinly in a piney wood, like that betwixt Passin Merrydith's and Ganwy's Mill, but heer is verry commun indeed and nuthin out'n the way. Is I sed befo, nun uv um aint finisht, not even the Captul, and pun top uv nearly all uv um thar is things sumthin like the big king-post to a sale vessil, only bigger, but mo like the figger 4 trigger to a imments pat rich trap, only wun peese are a roap instid up wood. But the bildins aint traps that I kno uv, ixcept to ketch munny, and thease heer big triggers is intendid to hiest rock. You've seen the like on a wrailrode; thar wuz wun at Bufflo Bridge. this side uv Fomvil. It ar custumerry fur strangers to go ferst to the Patint Offis, which I went along, uv koas, and seen sites I tell you—two or three milyuns uv curostics frum all parts uv the gloab, and a heap mo moddils uv masheens, all in glas casis. Berds and beests, munkis and snaiks, rocks and figgers, and pictchers, and evvrything doun to ole Genrul Washintun's solgir close, and skreech owils and aags. Ded peepil too, and heds cut off, and humin bones, horryfine to behole.

The mornin I wer up thar, Mr. Oans he wer thar, and I warnt akwaintid with him then, but follerd long behine, apeerintly without intendin it, becaze he wuz with sum ladies and what they all sed ixplained things to me. Peard like the ladies, wun uv um, wuz mitey smart and yumrus, laffin and makin Mr. Oans laff, in his dont keer way, at what she sed. I coodint begin to tell you wun haf uv it all, but wun thing I wer bleest to remember, it struck me so foasbly. Goin roun wun uv the glass casis, she remarkt—

"Law, Mr. Oans, doo cum heer, and look at this."

He went roun, and I heer him inquier. He says:

"Well, what is it?"

She sais, talkin like a little chile, jes lernin:

"Why," she sais, "jes look doun thair at them mair's aags—aint they mair's aags?"

"Ashoridly," he sais, "and ef you wuz to tern wun uv um over, it wood be a colt's revolver."

Then they all bust out a laffin gredidgus, but I diddint sea no cents in it. Presinly they went on, and I went roun and lookt. Sho nuf, it wer a aag big nuf to be a mar's aag, (a hoss mar, I meen,) but I dont bleeve wun werd uv it. I nuvver sean no mar settin on no ness hatchin no colts, and you nuther.

They all walkt on into the masheen room, whar they diddint stay long, but lef me thar lookin at the wheals, and spokes, and jigamarigs untwell my hed farly whirld. Arfter keerful igsaminashin, I coodint say I thought much uv enny uv thease invenshins, which posbly sum uv um may be verry good fur the present. I went away frum thar, but go thar okashunly when

I git loansome, which Mr. Oans he sais a pawnbroker. (whatuvver that is,) is verry apt to be loansome. All this tiem you may be certin I wer keepin a sharp look out fur my bizniss. Wun tiem, I had a grate mine to tell Mr. Argruff, but arfter wreflecktin tho't I'd better sey nuthen too soon. Neether hav I menshind ennythin to enny uv our Ferginny Kongissmun, which I've bin interjuiced to, Mr. Letchur, Mr. Bocox frum our deestric, Mr. Powl, Mr. Edmund's sun, Mr. Clemmings, Jedge Casky, and them; all wise, kine hartid gentilmen, willin to do enny thing fur you they ken. Sum uv um I got akwaintid with befo I lef Broun s tavun, wun day when I wer takin sperrits, pritty good too, heap bettern that at the Junkshin, with Mr. Argruff. They jined verry perlitely, and, heerin whar I wer frum, commenst on pollytix, askin how I stood. You know how a good drink takes the bashful out uv a fello, so I torked rite up to them grate Kongissmen jis like I wood to peepil baun and raisd at erost rodes. I tole um I wer a outenout, ole fashin, strait up and doun, staits rite, Jacksin, Kansis dimmokrat, bleevin in nuthin but whut the party bleevd in, votin fur a dimmokrat aginst enny boddy, I doant keer hoo.

"That's rite," they sais, " you stick to that, and doant truss too much to yo oan idees and you'll alwais be rite."

I sais, "I thank you," and we all mendid our drinks, and I want nigh as bashful as I wer at fust. So I assd um a questchin which had botherd me mitely, soon arfter I got to Washintun whar evvry boddy torks pollytix and you's bleeged to heer mo or less uv what they tork about. I sais:

"Gentilmen, sense I cum heer, evvry boddy a most is acusin uv evvry boddy uv bein uv a dimmy gog; what ar a dimmy gog, ar it a kind uv dimmokrat or a vessil that holes licker?"

This apeerd to amews um mitely, and wun sed, laffin, that my urror wer verry commun, becos it aint evvry man which knows the diffrens between a dimmy gog and a dimmokrat."

He sais, speakin to me, S'e, "The true diffrents is verry simple, and kin be ixplained in a breth. Whoever gits electid is a dimmy gog, and whoever gits defeatid is a paytrlot. D'you understan?"

I tole him "sertny," but, I sais, "I've heerd thease heer

dimmy gogs abused so much and the Gnashnul dimmokrats abused so much, that I begun to think they wuz the same thing identikilly."

"Oh no!" he sais, "you must by no meens entertane sech apinyun. The Gnashnul Dimmockracy, altho they've bin electid and hole the powur uv guvvunmint, air not dimmy gogs; they air ixcepshins to the genril rool; they air the grate party, and however troo it may be that the party is sumwhut dividid Noth and South, yet air they inknucksorubbly conjined together by this verry divishin, and stronger than they wood be without it."

I had to studdy over this sum tiem befo I cood unnerstan how a thing cood be jined by a divishin. At lass I sais:

"I think I sea thoo yo observashin. The Gnashnul Dimmockracy uv the Noth and the South air jined together like the rooms in a jale—by a thik, unpassibul rock wall betwixt um. Uv koas the jale ar stronger fur the wall."

"Ixackly," he sais, "you've hit the nale rite on the hed."

I sais, "Well, I'm prowd uv sich a strong party," and so I am Billy, and you too.

He sais, "Well you may be, fur it's the only party that kin save the Yuneyun, and that's its bizniss."

"Yes," I sais, "and it remines me powfully uv a song I reckin all uv you gentilmen have heerd befo now—a nigger song, but full uv meenin, calld,

> 'Ef you have enny goodin thing,
> Save it, save it;
> Ef you have enny goodin thing,
> Save *me* sum!'"

They all walkt off up stars in a roe uv lafter. I reckin I'm a gittin to be a rite funny man, or probly they laff at me becos they think I'm a fool. I dunno.

I intendid in this letter to uv tole you about my fust vissit to Kongiss, but kinnot.

Give my luv to Patsy Allin, yo sister Betsy and Fanny and all.

Yo fren and cussin,
MOZIS ADDUMS.

FOURTH LETTER.

THE MINTZPI HOUS—A KONVERSASHIN—MR. ADDUMS VISITS KONGISS.

Dear Billy:

We all, that is me and Oans and Melloo and Mr. Argruff, bodes at the Mintzpi Hous, which the pies thar aint made uv the kommin mint, but jedgin fum thar tace uv peppurmint, with a leetle injun tunnups and frakshin of dekade colluds. They has um evvry day, regly. My idee uv a pi, ar appil dumplint. Pottpi aint bad, pervidin you doant hav no surplis uv hog fatt and bacin rines, sich as yo ant Polly ar invayubbly boun too hav. Pankakes with good, thik, blak, Alleendz mlassis, is splendid.

As regards the other eetin thar at the Mintzpi Hous, taint much. Not a crum uv konbred I've techt senst heer I've bin. They brings to the tabil a kind uv battur-bred, which it ar certny ar spuyus. Billy if you cood send me a good hot pone with olefashin cruss, hard is the devvil, which it eets and look like a pees uv brokin skillit, givin uv a man's jor-teath sum rashnul and holesum exursies, you'd do me a faver. Ef you had a Kongissmun thar to franc it, you cood jess rop it up in a newspapir and send it rite along. Francing ar a Kongissmun ritin uv his name on enny thing, which it then goes free in the Postoffis all over kreashin. I wondir when the Kongissmuns gits on the car they doant rite thar naim on thar oan bax, and go grattis. But you sea govunmint is sech a fool it pais um fur cummin, calling uv it mielidge. Billy, spose you was to hi a man to doo sum dichin, and was to pay him a hevvy pries fur doin uv it; woodint you think he wer distracktid ef he wuz to ass you to pay him extry fur cummin to whar he cood git too his wuk? Uv koas. When I lived ovsee fur Doctellick Dillin, I walkt ten miel in the wrain to git thar, and the idee of chargin him nuthin fur goin thar, nuvver entud my hed. I'd a thot I wuz a fool ef it had. But such is Kongiss. Oans tells me thar's a Sennytur here in Washintun which has bilt him a puffick pallis with wun trip of mile money. And a member from Jorjy has bilt him a hole toun with the saim, which for the reesin he calls it Mileidgevil.

At the Mintzpi, which Oans—hees a funne fello, he calls it the Mintpizin Hous, sayin he bleeves they ceezins the pize thar with ossnick—thar's a whole chanse of boders, a heep uv um ladies, old and yung, pritty and ugly, prinsipilly hoamly, marrid and singil. I tell you, they dressis outin the ashis. Caliker? I aint sean a stich, I aint smelt caliker, wunst over thar. They doant mine nuthin. Arms bar up to the arm pitts, nakes nakid, free is ar. Ded uv wintur, too: sno on the groun, thurmonitur doun to zeeroe. By-jing! I wondir what wimmin's skins is maid uv. I'me be dad shimd ef they wuz jess tand ef they woodint maik the warmmist kine uv shoo that uvver wuz wo. Kin cole pennytrait um? It kin sertny not. Then agin, thees heer ladis, drest so nise, is monsus keerful uv thar close, histin thar kotes hi and fer up in wet wether, not shamed nor feard of whats thar.

A numbo, in fac most uv thees ladis I dunno ; a few I duz, mo ptickly Miz Hanscum, which her husbun hees gone to Kallyforny, and Miss Saludy Trungil, which shees a verry grait fren uv Oans and Melloo, and Mr. Argruff okashinully ingagis her in konversashin lait at nite. Miz Hanscum shees powful pritty, powful, and so eesy to git akwainted with, being afecshinit I jedge. They say shees mitey writch, and I reckin its soe, fur she wars a site uv joolry uv the finest kine. Miss Saludy Trungil, shees a remarkably stylish looking gearl, bein tall, handsum formd, full uv cents, and a leetil sassy I ixpec. She and Oans is mitey thick. Mr. Argruff, he injoize her, and evin this heer kuyus, punkin-faistid littil Melloo, he grins orful at her sumtiems. Shees boun to be smart. At a nuther tiem I shill tell you how I cum to no thees ladis.

Uv koas thar's a large passil uv gentilmen at the Mintzpi—Sennytuz, Wripryzentativs, Ginruls, Jedgis, Clux, and so foth, with thar wievs and dorters, tho the clux they cant afode to hav no wievs, bein retchid po, they tell me. Billy, it ar wuth a man's while, which has bin used to commun plantashin igzistents to cum in heer to thees tremenjus tavun bildins, with their marvil floes, splenkid parlus, and bewtiful carpits to see the fine foax, and speshilly the ladis, sailin long the passagis heer and at Brouns, and the Gnashnul and Willud's They rarr back so prowd! They has sich hoops, they goe by you so skonful, and the soun uv thar cilks and sattins skrapes yo verry nurves, makin uv the skin uy yo boddy krorl and yo ize uv yo hed to git dark with a swimmy-fine mist at the site of so much magniffiysent frock surroundin wun littil woman, which you cant bleeve she blongs to the famly of Addum and Eave, baun to sin and sorro. No Billy, thees proud cretus is liftid hi abuv mawtallity, and, seein uv um, you stands thar cole in your goose-skin aflictid with a abominable cents uv infeyorrity. Jess fur the saik uv the ixsperrymint, you feal like youd like to taik wun uv thees gloyus beans into a pees uv ploud groun and pull a fisshin worrum out uv whar its jess bin turned over by the mole bode and put it rite into the pam of her littil white han. You warnt to cumpar what's in her han with the han itself, and then flosfize upon the subjict.

 Me and Oans and Melloo was talkin bout this heer verry thing the uther nite in Oan's wroom, and Mr. Argruff he cum in while we wuz kunversin and evury wunst in a whiel techin sum uv the finist kine uv Robsin County, Tennysy, whiskey which Hon. Mr. Joans he give to Oans. I wremarked pritty much what I has giv you abuv, and Oans, (which ar the kuyasist yung man in the wirld, bein puffickly retchid inside uv a hous with his close on, strippin uv um off to the white under wuns soon's he gits in his wroom) Oans he sais "Mozis," wee's vay familyar now, " Mozis," he sais, "you doo great injestis to the far secks uv Washintun sitty. Soe far frum not likin fishin worrums, thay ar verry fond uv um. Dont you know that thay taiks um and bleechis um and cooks um and eets um?"

 "Shuh!" I sais, "you cant fool me."

 S'e "Its a fac, I asho you. Thay jess cuts off the cens uv um and eets um. Thay ar wun of the mose fashnubble dishes uv polisht suckles, and the Frentch naim fur um is mackaroney."

 I lookt at him, and seen his kountinunts were intily cumposed. Then I wundud at the humin nacher uv fine drest wimmin in sittis which eets fishin worrums and call um by the naim which Yankee Doodil called his poney. And I has senst lernt that fashnubbil peepil eets musheroons, esteamin uv um uv a grate dellikissy. Littil, ole Melloo ar a cole-bloodid po cretur, and when he sets in a rume stranddils rite roun a stoav, like it wuz a littil nigger boy he wuz drawin in tween his laugs to pat him on the hed. He doant say no mitey much, and akordin what he duz say souns mo'n what it is, caws its rar. He spoak up.

S'e "The Buckingame man, (mec, you kno, Billy) ar rite. All wimmin ar dirt. The identitty's absloot. I shood like to see Addumsis ixperrymint tride. Dirts vary. Sum's good and sum's bad, sum's wirth cultervaytin and sum aint. And I reckin Addums ean tell us what the farmus put in dirt to improve it."

S'I "Menyo, gorno."

S'e "Igzactly. The sitty sivlizashun uv wimmin is but the adawnment uv so mutch oridginal femail mud with a cantankeruss crop uv silks and ribbins foaced up by the stimmulus uv gold, the only troo soshil and plittykill gorno."

"Cum," sais Mr. Argruff, "this ar verry wrong talk for men who has mothers and sisters. None uv you bleeve a wird you say. Mozis here is verry yung"—

"Well," I sais, "I'm tollibul yung both in ears and ixspeyunts, but I'm 20 and considerbil upuds."

"Well," s'e "when you git to be is ole is I am, you'll bee mo charrytubble. Theas yung ladis ar vane. But evvry-boddy is vane"—

"Yes," I sais, "all is vannyty seth the preechur."

"Peepil maik a distinkshin," he kontinyud, not mindin me, "betwean vannyty and pride, praisin wun and pretendin to dispies the uther. It's troo, fur mettyfisicul pupposis, they kin be sepratid, but, in point of fac, they are wun and the saim thing —the saim impults actin in diffrint dreckshins. Konshus powur; that's it. Ejeckt it apun the boddy, it is vannyty; infews it intoo the sperritt, it's pried. Bewty is womun's power; yes, and man's too. Pried is sed to be the basis of ambishin, and ambishin the movin foase uv the soldjer and the staitsmur. But you nuvver sor a grate woryur or emnent staitsmun who was'nt at hart a thousan tiems mo vane then the vanist gearl that sweeps the floes uv Broun's pollus as tho she wuz Klepattry, and had Seezur and Antny and Roam and Ejipp, eye! the hole wirl at her feat."

"Good!" sayes Oans.

"Robsin Kounty whisky," sayes Melloo.

Mr. Argruff, he went on, sayin uv:

"And Mozis complanes uv thar skon. But skon is nuthin but a nuther naim for ignorunts, which indead ar the jenerrick turm for awl humin foltz. Wimmen and men only skon thoes hoom thay doant no, or hoom they reely kunsider unwirthy.

"Thar is wimmin at Broun's and the Gnashnul and the Mintzpi, hoo think so meenly uv me that my presintz maiks no impreshin on thar auguns uv vishin—they can't posbly sea mee. Butt kneethur the man nor the womun evver breatht the breth of life hoo cood skon me after wunst I hav walkt camly up to the doughs uv thar soles and knockt. And I'll wajur that the proudist lady in Washintun will luv Mozis Adduins arftur she cums to noe him. Wimmen fantsy wild felloes, but they ar compeld by a lor uv thar nachur to *luv* sich men as Mozis. In all thar silk and jooils they wood be glad to sea him in his hoamspun close; thar harts spontaingusly goes out to meat an honist, simple-minded, unsuspishus cretur like him."

"But," I sez, "I ar suspishus—spishus is the devvil, and I've got good close is ennyboddy in my trunc, but I'm not a gointer war um evvry day. Then agin flatrin a man too his fais is bad mannus, I didnt keer how well twuz ment."

"Well, we wont quorl a bout that," he sais. "I beg yo pardin. But you doo our Washintun gearls injestis. Didge evvur goe with the gearls on a fisshin frollick, Mozis?"

"Imfatkly I has," I sais.

S'e "wuzzint it plesint?"

"It were prime," I sais.

S'e "No dout. And you foun yo gearls wuz jest is pritty and sweete way off in the woods and by the watus is they wuz at hoam in the drawn room. Its jess so with thees gearls heer. Taik um out in the kuntry and you'll fine they ar is natchrul thar is a tree or a blaid uv grass. The fac is, Mozis, a gearl is like a sac cote; she fits enny boddy, or ruther I shood say any plais."

Then he stopt, and side, and kept silent.

"Goe on," sais Oans.

I sais the saim.

Melloo, handin doun the bottil uv Tennysy whisky sais, "taik a littil uv the sperrits uv bad men maid perfeck."

Mr. Argruff filld him up a squerril lode and wrezumed.

S'e "I'm a retchid man—a retchid man. And all becoz uv a dreem which I had it fotty senchris ago, and has evver sintz bin trine to realize it. In vane! I've but wun wish in this life, and my prar is this. Sum sweet, bloo summer day, the sweetist that evver dornd, I wish to spend aloan under the trees and by the wortus with the most bewtifull wummun in the wirl. We must be abslootly aloan, and we must be togethur all day, frum the risin uv the sun to the goin doun uv the saim."

"What!" sayes Oans, "without enny thing to eet? Fo fride ("meenin oshters, you no Billy) by all meens—fo apeece."

"No," I sais, "sum fride chickin, buttud biskits, and a fisshin lien."

Mr. Argruff, he went on like he nuvver heerd nun uv us. "While the lite lasts, let me look deap intoo the hevvin uv her ize and listen to the music uv her vois. When the day trimbles in deth, and when the sun sens his last wred shaft from the purpal hills, let me press my lips to her oan, and let that last sunray be a javlin uv fier te kunsoom me thar, utt'ly, soe that I shall becum soe muich blank spais; fer ef evin wun pottikil uv my mateyul boddy remaned, the memry uv that day uv blis wood wrevivvyfy and ixpand it intoo a senchent sole, kapebil uv the pane uv longin fer that whitch cood cum agin no mo frevver, or ef it kaim, wood not be whut ferst it wuz."

Oans seamed techt, and sed heed had that idee ofting. Little ole Melloo sais very sarkastick, "Argruff, lemme advies you to set up a retale poitry shop. 'Git a masheen, and werk it with Rob'sin County Whisky."

I sayes, "Mr. Argruff, did you think you wuz marrid to that ar gearl?"

"No," he sais, strong.

"Well," I wremarkt, "unlest I wuz marrid too her, I ruther sumboddy shood be thar. The ginrul apinyun uv the naberhood"—

"Dam the naberhood!" he wreplied, "thar's no naberhood in the kais."

With that the argymint drapt, and we all squandud off to our sevril apartmints.

I has give you this a kount, Billy, not becaus I deams the idee uv settin on the bank uv a kreak all day with a gearl ar ennything verry aridginul or calculatid to instruck you mutch, but becaus it shose you how wremakabul is the mines uv the peepil of Washintun. Cert'ny evrything and evryboddy heer is strandge, and, as Mr. Argruff sais, *sui genris*, which is the latten fer peckewlyer. Uv the akewaintuntsis I has lately maid, nun is mo intrestin an taukativ than Mr. Hicmun, which hees vulg'ly called Bo, tho' I've nuvver sean him with a lady yit. He chargis a quarter uv a dollur to be intojuiced to you, and runs his tung like a wheet fan, like he wuz feerd you woodint let him git throo. His face is fross bit and rinkled powful, and hees got him a sharp, onnachrul eye. I nuvver seas him, which I do sea him mos evry day, hobblin long the street with his shorl, and his stripid britchis, and his bung'd-up feat, but my reckoleckshun terns to too things neer Kerdsvil, which is this:

Ole Capin Sinker had him a hoss, naim Wrankin, wunst a fien saddil hoss, but bein mitey ole, terned him outen a ole feel to die, in the naberhood uv a ole tumbil doun terbarker hous. He had plenty to eet, but what he eet dun him no good, and he goot leener and leener every day, till you cood uv hangd a hat on his hipp boans, is they say. Whenuvver ole Wrankin lade doun, which was ofting, the buzzuds got arfter him, atacting him, dartin at him, and peckin at his ize. Finely po ole Wranpin suffred so mutch from these onslots he got nurvus, and ef a clowd cum over the sun he thot it wuz the shadder uv a buzzud in the ar, and went intoo the terbarker hous and shet the dough to keep fum bein eet befo his tiem. Well, wun day it cum close clowdy all day, and po ole Wrankin thinkin the hevvins wuz alive with buzzuds, staid in his terbacker hous, and shet the dough, and thar dide, and bout nite cum a clap uv thunder, nockt doun the ole hous, berrid him, and maid a fine monyumint fer him. Well, Mr. Hicmun wremines me of that ar ole skragly ole hoss and that ar ole tumblin-doun ole hous, which methinx he can't hole up long. He ar sertny ar a man uv jeenyus, whitch I feals a fealin uv simp'thy fer him.

I seas, Billy, I'm libel to run offn the trac is a injine on the Sowthsied wrail-rode, as I hassint tole you uv nuthin hardly I begun to tell you uv. But wun thing mo I must knarate year I quits this heer epistul which ar is follers:

I tellin Mayan I had a grate seckret, which I fines I can't keep nuthin frum her uv my oan, shee idviesd me not to truss noboddy, not eavin Mr. Argruff, and p'tickly Oans and Melloo, which she sais they nose two mutch ennyhow; but too tend too my oan afars myself. So I thot I'd nock aroun and taik pusnul observashin uv evrything, speshly uv Kongiss. So I gose and gose way up the streat in the mist of a grate dust which blose heer konstunt like thrashin uv wheet, and gose up too the Captul. I jes tell you the Captul heer ar a nuther site to the Captul in Richmun, but the yard, which its fashnubble to call it grounds in a sitty, ar about pritty mutch the saim, sicks uv wun and haf duzzen uv the uther. The bildin ar about is long is frum Baldin's ole sto (thay tells me hees dun move doun to the planc rode) too the Piskypil cherch in Kerdsvil. Speekin to Oans a bout this bildin he sais its like awl gall, devided intoo thee parts. But I tole him that a gall were wun thing, whitch it wuz a blarther.

"Ah," he sais, "but, you sea, I sed awl gall; awl gall ar a difrint thing frum gall; awl gall ar a Frentchmun's gall, whitch its totely difrint from a Emerrykin's gall, bein heap mo uv it; and that's the resin Frentch peepil is the mose gall-ant in the wirl." And thar ar a spesmin uv wun uv Oansis punz (pun, meenin a wird whitch meens sumthin eltse) on the wird glant, whitch is spry, tentive to the gearls.

Howuvver, the Captul bildin heer ar imments. Taint finisht tho, and the top uv the middel uv it ar adauned with a surkil uv pillers whitch bein part white and part black, looks like trees whitch has bin beltid, sum beltid and sum burnt. You has to go up a site uv steps to git intoo the bildin, and the ferst thing you cums to ar a marvel monyumint, representin nakid humin beeins standin roun a post whitch has a numbo uv split pitchers stuck to the sides uv it—and this monyumint are bilt rite in the middel uv a pon uv stagnint warter, rite grean; and what's mo the pon warnt thar oridginully, but wus maid thar to bild the monyumint in. You wont bleeve me, Billy, but its the fac, and shows what fool peepil thar is in this wirl. Thar's a iun railin roun the pon, and when I lookt over it intoo the pon, I sean the cook had been thorin slops intoo it, p'tickly carrots. But twarnt carrots, Billy; what you reckin twuz? Why, gole fish, whitch the pon is ful uv um, and thay lade so still in the warter I thot twuz carrots. Gole fish is a kine uv yaller belly pearch, only thar backs is yaller, or ruther wred, too.

While I wus a lookin at the pearch, fine ladies and membus uv Kongiss kep on passin me goin up stars intoo the parler, whitch is alwais in the secund story, the parler is in toun. Fealin moddis, I detummined to go in the kitchin and chat with the kook, whitch I hoped she wus a fatt ole nigger womun, like a kook orter be, tel I wus envitid up stars with the cump'ny. I past on by a marvil tombstone runnin warter under the bridge, got intoo the hous and lookt and lookt fer the kitchin, which dernd ef I cood fine it. I ass'd a man goin by totin uv books, but he pade no atenshun to me. I tride a heap uv doughs; all lockt. Finely, I thot I'd go up stars ennyhow, and went up, and when I got thar it lookt mo like doun stars than doun stars did. Peerd like twuz a seller, with big dubbel posses uv rok, and a skewpt out scalin, and heap uv bocksis, and trash, and wun thing and a nuther layin about. Peepil wuz passin, a few uv um, but not likin to ixpose my igronunce, I sais nuthin to um. It were rite dark in thar, and I went aroun and aroun twell pren'ly I cums to whar it were lighter, and ternin throo a glass dough, foun a par of twistid steps goin up hier yit in the bildin. I wus a goin on up, but hapnin to look over my shoulder I sean a nuther glass dough, and throo it peepil, which I node it were Kongiss. Aproachin the dough, a m'latter man settin inside halls it rite opin with a roap, and I goes in uv koas, fealin prity imbarist, and not seein uv mutch fer a tiem. When I cum too a little, I sean a small room, with a hollo sealin runnin up in a kcervd maner, mogny fernitcher, a few peepil, and roun the room at reglar pints, a numbo uv busters uv grate men. Buster ar the likeniss, hed, fase, neck, and pees uv the bress uv a man, chopt out uv white marvil, with a bottum part sumthin like the bottum uv a wine glass, to set it on. Behine a long, levil, mogny bannister, set sum uv the kuyustist humins in exzistunts. Of all and uv all, they wuz the beet. Ugly? Blessed farthers! I shood jedge they wuz; and ole, and rinkildy, and drest in black silk apuns, with tremendus sleaves, settin thar behine that ar bannister, still is deth. Yuve sea sevin nor ate mud turkils squottid on a log, and yuve sea sevin nor ate ole tukky buzzuds settin on a lim of a tre; well that is pecisely like them ole felloes settin behine that ar bannister.

A gristly kine uv a man wuz a standin on the flo in frunt of sum tabils, trine to pint out a fac or ixplain sumthin ruther to them ole turkils and buzzuds, which they did'nt taik no intruss in what he sed, 'pearin to be sleap mostly, but sum uv um readin. I shood uv hav jedged the man on the flo to be a loryer ef he hadin bin so eesy and natchrul like—he did'n rar nor he did'n rip, nor beller, nor rampooge, nor tar his shert—he warnt a bit like our loryers which I has sean plenty uv um at Buckingame kote. I tride and tride to compren whut this fello on the flo wus a sayin; but all I cood doo I coodin taik no mo ingziety in it then the mud turkils afosed.

"And this ar Kongiss," I sais to myself. "Well, dern Kongiss," and I lef.

Goin out by the glass dough which the m'latter man he pulled open agin with his string, I cums at the foot uv the windin stars, to a ole man sellin appils, caikes, pize, and so foth. I bot a par uv pize, and ass'd fer sumthin to drink. The ole man sed he did'n had nuthin but sum logger beer.

"Ennything like p'simmun beer?" I sais.

He did'n seam to understan me, so I sais:

"Gimme sum ennyhow." And he gimme sum, and I tastid it, and it jess squirtid itself spontaniyusly outin me all over him, saim is ef I'd bin a surrindge.

"No wunder yew calls it logger beer," I sais, fuyus; " ef it taint stump warter I wisht I may be dad shimd," whitch it ar, Billy. And I lef.

What mo I sean uv Kongiss I resurves. I've rit anuff fer wun tiem, certin.

Luv to Unc' Jim. 'Member mee to Kayine and An' Locky.

Wrispeckfully and afeckshuntly yose.

MOZIS ADDUMS.

FIFTH LETTER

MOZIS ON KANSAS. INSIDE VEIW OF POLITICAL LIFE. MIZ HANSCUM AND MAYAN.

DEAR BILLY:

Billy that warnt no Kongiss I seen, twarnt nuthin but the Spreame Kote, which I shood uv knode it in a minnit ef that ar loryer hader hiseted the saddil skeerts uv his mentil anemil and socked the rowels uv his vois intoo the intestins uv his argymiet as is the fashin uv the mo notid as well as uv the yung and asspirin membus uv the wroorul bar. Uv the reeul Kongiss thar is a par uv um, bein 2, wun small wun calld Sennit, and wun bigg wun calld Hous. But lets furst igzamin the struckcher uv the Spreame Kote of the Yewnited Staits uv Emerryky, which it shall bee a breef expositchun, quite breef.

You buy a par uv plow lines from—we'll say Ned Sinker in Fomvil. They terns out to be wrottin in the twiss, and you refusis to pay fer um. You git sude, and jedgemint goes agin you. You apeals, and the sute goes on frum Kote to Kote, hier and hier, untwell it gits way heer into the Spreame Kote, sichyewatid under the Washintun Kongiss bildin, as afosed. Thar it stops, it's got too the verry lass knotch on the beem uv the mighty stilyuds uv Jestis. Nine humin turkils in silk gounds takes the kais in hand, and when they've sed thar say, nuthin mo kin be sed, you got to shet up, pay fer yo ole wuthless, ole plow lines, and a heap mo besldes. At lees this ar Mr. Argruff's explaynashun which he giv it too me sune arftur the advencher wrelated in the finis, the eend uv a formur epissill.

As to Kongiss, to retern. Thar's a par uv um, Hous and Sennit. Ef wun ar calld Hous, the uther orter be calld Hut or ruther Volt, sais Oans, becos Sennit ar a meen littil goudgdout darkey hole, wharas Hous ar a wrisplendid and imments apartmint, got up without wregard to coss, and full of the finis paint and gildin, jined together in the mose startlin and ixquizit tace, saim is a writch, a brite and a brillyunt quilt, which a stewjus ole made in the kuntry, havin a igzistunts littruily bloated with spar time, she maiks it, and sens it, with menny aintchunt and varginul teers, and fond hoaps uv glowry, to the Anyul Farr at Richmun, whar it taiks the pries or doant taik it, akordin too the mo or less pewterifide cents uv the bewtyfull uv the Kummitty on quiltz fer the time bein. Thus seth Oans, and I fobar to add nuthin to the crittycism.

Sence heer I've bin, I've bin to Kongiss a menyer time, and ef I has lernt ennything, which I has my douts uv it, it ar this. Ef uvver I doo cum to Kongiss, which I shill nuvver do it is long is I kin mall rails or eet persimmuns, the fust thing I intends to doo ar pintidly to interjuice a nact to amend a nact that nuvvur wuz intitled a nact to permote the efecshincy uv Kongiss; fur uv all peepil on the fais uv the erth to tauk, and tauk, and tauk, and do nuthin, they is the beet.

And Kanzis, Billy—goodness nose I wisht it wuz berrid under Willisis mountin. I doo think it's enuf to maik a man cuss out and quit the humin famly which has heerd what I has heerd on this drottid subjick; constunt, Billy, without no sessashin furuvver and furuvver mo. Nar a tiem has I gone to Kongiss but straitway a man upriz and pode foth the viles uv his rath on Kanzis, howlin at it like a houn when you blow the hon fer dinner, yelping at it like a fice when he seas a straindge nigger cummin in the yard.

But I stans by my party in this heer matter, Billy. The gloyus dimmockrasy and Mister Wilyum Cannun (I hates the vulgly way uv callin uv him Mr. Buck Cannun) is rite, puffickly rite in thar psitshun.

But I feals mitey bad about this Kanzis enny way, and the kuntry too. Things is cum to sich a pass that we ar ableged to cary on the guvnurmint and exekcut the lors, under falts pretensis as twuz; we cant doo what we kno to be rite ixcep int he naim uv them we kno to be doin rong, and the grate hoss cart of public afars is a gointer to stall pritty soon. It's bin a travlin uv a mitey ruff rode lattly ennyway, the tail-bode is busted, and the most vallybil kontents is a joltin out wun arfter anuther powful fast. Befo long, I'm afeard Mr. Wilyum Cannun will fine his horses is goin too fast, and lookin roun to sea what's the reesin, will fine the waggin-boddy intlely empty, the lode all gone cleen.

In Hous and Sennit, from time to time, I've sea the mos distinguisht men up the nashin, and bin astonisnt at thar close resemblunts to the rest of mankine. But menyer grate man livs in a common hous, like Unc Jim for igsampil; so tis with the soles of jeenyus, which most in ginrully speakin dwells in tennymints, badly bilt at ferst, and soly in knead uv new wetherbodin, white-wash, an mo brix on top uv the chimblys to bring um up to the standud uv graujer.

I has sed thar is a close resemblunts between Kongismen and and human nacher is you find it laying about ennywher. To be kandid, Billy, they is wun and the saim thing, identykil wripresentatives and men is. Git jam up aginst um, you can't tell um apart to save yo life you can't.

I wuz struck with this remokabul fac freakwently when I has went into Honnerbul Mr. Swomplansis room, and a pompus and mo kunseetid ole fool than ole Swomplans nuvver had pockits in a kote tail. Pusnally hees igzackly like Littleberry Huddilstun, igsept his head ar ball, but his caetur ar a mixtur uv Ganwy's Yawk and Bell. Now tuther nite.

Thar wuz thar in ole Swomplans' room three or fo yung Kongismun, and bewchiful spesmins they wuz. Nuvver in all my born dais did I heer sech cussin an swarrin and tellin uv joaks. They got to runnin wun nuther about their rekods. You sea, Billy, soon's a man gose into pollitix everything he sais and duz is kep akount uv, and that akount is called reekod. So ef a pollytishun duz ennything rong, his ennymis goes to his reekod and pints out the fac, and the very plais and time whar he dun it, and has got to tell mo lies than anuf to get shet uv it So when they wuz all a talkin bout this, yung Mr. Joans he ups and swo he had the damdis mos butyfull reekod on erth. Then yung Bosin ript out and sed he wisht he may be teetotally swept into —— ef *his* reekod warnt p'yo* and spotliss is the senter page uv the sacrid album uv a virgin's sole. "D— it," sais Joans.

* Pure.

"how'd you vote on the Kanzis-Nebrasky bill? "And cuss you, diddin you maik a speech lass Summer in favur uv distributin the proseeds uv the public lans? You ar no better than an infunnil No-Nuthin ennyhow," ansers Bosin. So they went rippin and cussin at each uther tell Swomplans he spoke up and tole um they wus compormisin the dignity uv Congreshnul carrickter. "What," sais he, "wood yo constitchyunts think ef they cood heer this undignifide, pofane, and vilent oltercashun?"

They both damd thar constitchyunts to the devil, and took a drink. They wuz cummensin at it agin, when little ole Melloo stopt um saying uv: "Gentmen, you ar both equilly grate, and yo reekods equilly immackulit, but listin to this." He red frum a paper heed bid ritin, which went on to say that a telegraf dispatch just resceeved frum the grate Dimmokratic Convenshun, then settin (imadjinin the year ateen-sixsty-ate) at Hayvanner in the Ilund uv Cuby, had anounst that eether the Rite Honnerbil Sennytur Bob Joans, or Guvner Tom Bosin had reeseeved the unanimus nominashun fer Pressydint.

"Uv koas you'll be electid," sais Melloo," "whichever gits it, and as things is goin on wun uv you will be boun to git it, and now I wanter know what you gointer doo for me yo ole and valyud fren and intmit kumpanyun?"

Bosin spok furst. He sais:

"I shall pursurve the dignity uv my stashin. I shall say, Mr. Melloo, I'm not unmincful uv the pass. I recall the plesint hows uv yuth, when we wus frens togethur, as I'm yose now. But I o it to my kuntry and myself to make my adminystrashun gloyus, and to that eend I inten to slekt for my constitewshunul advisers, and for the princepell wripresentatives uv the wripublick abroad, the verry ferst men in the knashin. My long akwaintunts with you will not justify me in assining enny uv thease psichins to Mr. Melloo. Nuvvertheless you shell hav a poss uv honnur and uv proffit. Whereupon I'll hand you yo commisshin as consul to Livpool or Peekin."

Then Joans sed: "You aint goin to hear no such stuff is that frum me. Soon's you call on me at the White Hous I am a gointer say, 'Peter,' (that Melloo's givin naim,) 'Peter, ole feller, how ar you. I'm d—d glad to see you. Taik a seet and set doun. Then I'll send for a bottle up green ceal, and we'll both git is drunk is d—. And befo you go way, I'm gointer say to you like Ole Buck sed to Forny, 'taik whutuvver you dam pleas.' And ef yu ar smart like Forny, and go in fur the publick printin, you shell hav it. I'm not goin to refuse you nuthin. It'll then be wuth about two milyuns a yeer, and ef we dont hav the tallest kind uv a time you may take my hat. We'll live like the Sardeens uv Annopolis,* becos I doant inten to git marrid, but I'm a gointer to have all the pritty wimmin in the Yunitid Statis bodin at the White House free uv charge; and we'll rip rite throo fo splendid yeers, certin and sho! Joans may talk about his adminnistrashin, but mine is gointer to leave behine it a streak of glowry long is tail uv a comic and brite is a flash uv litenin. That's so. You may bet yo life on it. The way for a man to maik his administrashin glowyus is to stan up to his frens like ole Jacksin and taik the responsibillity. Twont do for a Pressydint to be squeemish and conshentshns. Conshents be d—d! Ole Buck's tride that gaim, and it deant pay "

Billy, thêm's his verry wurds. It's true he ware yung, both Joans and Bosin, but they ar upun a par with the ballunce, jest is smart and smarter than wun haf uv um. And that's the way grate men, Dimmocrats and all, go on when they ar by themselves talkin bout thar kuntry, thar Pressydent, and the responsibil duties uv thar station like it warnt nuthin. Doant you say a wurd about this, you heer. Ef uvver it wus to git out, the kuntry wood be ruined, ruinatid. Nuvver no members uv Kongiss wood cum heer no mo. Hoo cood truss um arftur talkin in that ar way? Why peepil in the kuntry, when they went to maik thar speechis at a preesink, wooddiut dar to come anigh um. Wood they, Billy?

Heer I've dun run away with mysef agin, like a ole hoss arfter sum mischifus boy hav put a cuckly burrer under his tail. But pollytix ar a subjict the mos prefoun, requirin abundunts uv time and spais fer the propper treatmint and elucydashun uv it. Ef brevvity are the sole uv witt, length are the upper-lether uv lojick, which my mine ar verry cleer on this pint tharof.

* *Can* Mr. Addams mean Sardanapalus?

I promist to tell you how I becum akwaintid with the ladis at he Mintzpi Hous, which the way uv it were in these wise. Wun day, goin in to dinner, my centsis compleatly absorbd in absents uv mine over the still mo futher puffeckshin uv my projick, rite at the dinin room dough I run agin Miss Saludy Tringil cummin a dantsin out as ushil, like a duck swimmin up to mill-wheel, and stumblin is I fell, I reecht out my han nachrilly to ketch sumthin, and getherd up sum tabil cloth and sum frock and sum cheer, which I think it muster bin the bac uv the saim, becos I upset Miz Hanscum backruds, brakin uv her plate and spillin uv a salt-seller in my eye. Thar it wuz befo the hole cumpny, and how I got out'n it I swar ef I kno. I nuvver shell git over it when I thinx uv it. I kno I diddent eat nuthin that day, and were shamed to go to tabil tel evryboddy had lef, tel laitly.

Oans—I doo like that Oans—he cum to me and cunsoled me, and when my mine grajually settled, tole me twuz my dewty to goe and apollygize like a gentmun. The perpriety wharof I perseevd at a glants. I assd him to give me a day to pepar my mine for the undertakin, and when the day were past and gone, with grate delibbyrashun and fumness I adrest myself to the task, and dun it. Jest befo I lef hoam on this expedishun you reckollect I got me the finis kine uv a sute uv clothes maid in Fomvil, which I reckin they ar cekul to enny maid ennywhar, I doant keer whar. Rambut fer coats, and Forrer fer britchis, the wirl cant beet um. And I had a par uv boots maid by Tony; kin mo be sed?

Araid in theese garmints, I felt like a gentilmun, which I ar in sperrit ef not in apeerunts, and, with the help uv Oans, made my apollogy soe satisfacktry, I soon becum a grate favrit with all the ladis, aspeshly Miz Hanscum—powful atracktiv womun she is, Billy. Arfter a modrit amount uv ixperrymints, I felt as nachrul in the Mintzpi parler is a steer in a patch uv clover. I vissitid thar freakwintly, and sumhow or ruther I were alwais thode with Miz Hanscum, which were the okashun wun nite uv this hapnin.

Didje ever hav a par uv dough-skin broad-cloth britchis, Billy? How slik they is. Well I had on mine that nite, and whenuvver I has um on I cant help slidin my hans doun um, it feals so good to the pam. Settin talkin to Miz Hanscum, she ubzervd my stroakin my britchis doun to the knees, like they wuz the nakes uv two blak hosses jes curry-combd and rubd down—ubservin this, it atracktid her attenshun, and she sais:

"Those apeer to bee verry nise pantloons, Mr. Addums."

"Yes'm," I sais, "Forrer maid um."

Then she assd me hoo Forrer wuz, and I tole her, and that indewsd her to queschin me sum mo, and mo yit, tel finely I giv her my hole histry. I reckin twuz levin o'clock befo I got thoo, and every body ware gone out'n the parler ixcept us, and we wuz settin plegg-takid clost together, she lookin so warm and good out uv her brite eyes like she reely keered for my welfar, and I fealin fine and puffickly kuntentid to stay rite thar, and ef ennything a lectil closter, tel day. Jest then, the dough opened and in cum Oans, evvydently not ixpecting to find noboddy. I spect he wanted to look at hisself in the long lookinglass they got thar runnin fum the flo clean up to the seelin. Ennyhow, the momint he seen us settin so intmit, he says quick "ixcuse me," and went rite out.

This kinder flustud me and I jumpt up, but Miz Hanscum she diddent mine it a bit, but sais in verry cam vois "set doun," and I set doun, and we went on talkin mo intmit than uvver. All uv a suddin, I jumpt up agin and sais "excuse me," and run out and diddent hardly stop runnin tel I got into my oan room.

"What maid me do so singly?" you sais.

Billy, she wuz arfter findin out my seakrit, shose you born she wuz!

You doant kno theese peepil in Washintun, and how keen they is arfter a vallybil thing. Haddint I heerd how the cunnin roskuls fum the North inveegils members uv Kongis with pritty ladis? You cant fool me.

To tell the truth, Billy, this acurrants hapened only lass nite, and I got a grate mine to stop bodin at the Mintzpi. It's danjus.

But this mornin I got up and tole Mayan the intire suckumunce, desirin to hav a intellijint veu uv a womun's doins fum anuther womun. Mayan were dustin the mantil pees when I cummenst a tellin her, and she ternd roun and listined good til I got clean thoo. Then she ternd roun and commenst dustin agin. I waited, but she diddent say nuthin. Gittin impaychunt, I sais:

"Warnt I rite in my conjeckshur?"

She kep on dustin, and sais in the mos keerless manner:

"It's no seekrit the pritty lady's afther a tall, a tall."

"She aint so mitey dog-gon'd pritty," I sais, "but what were she after then?"

And reckin, Billy, she diddent say she were arfter *me*. That bewtifull, writch Miz Hanscum arfter me! The idee! Then I reekollectid Mr. Argruff sayin how all the ladies in Washintun wuz bleest to luv Mozis Addums, the bar cunsepshun uv which giv me a pane in the eye-ball uv astonishtment. Verily, the wirld are straindge. Then I remembud the disparrity uv our suckumunsis in life, *at present*, and sais out loud,

"Sher!"

But Mayan she went on rubbin uv the mantil pees—she dun rubd it all over two three times aready—not notesin me in the leese. Jest then my eye lit upun her han, and consoun me, Billy, ef it warnt the prittiest, littlist, whitist, well-formed han in the wirld.

S'I, "Mayan. Look heer. Thar's sumthin rong about you. That aint no servunt gearl's han. That aint no han customd to werk."

Soon's I sed it, she snacht her han away like a bee had stung it, and hid it. Facin roun, she lookt at me white is a sheet, movin her lips, but sayin nuthin. Culler begins cummin to her check, yusully verry rosy, and she broke out:

"Mozis Addums, you is the biggis goos in the wirld," an she fled, and wuz doun stars in a minnit.

The sentents abuv, she sed it in the verry bess uv Inglish, like me and you speeks it, and it starkled me. I jumpt up and run arfter her, callin her:

"Mayan, Mayan," I sais.

"Surr," she wreplide, from way doun the steps. It cum up

coas is the teeth uv a whip-sor, and it hert me that bad I went and set doun on the bed for a nour befo I gits over it.

Billy, thar's sumthin rong about that gearl you may be boun, and I'm not a gointer res tel I finds it out. I shood uv hav rit you this letter long ago but fer the arivil heer uv Oans' par, a scrowgin ole gentmun, long amost is the toe-line uv a canel, havin uv ruther a pleasin fais all kivered with har, and runnin all over toun like he was distracktid, and me and Oans kontinyul runnin arfter him in a state uv painful mentil inziety and ankwish, fer feer heed loss himself or git hert. Peepil ort reely to be mo keerful how they low thees ole creturs to buss loos frum the wristraints uv the famly and fiside, and ixpose himself to the temtashins uv fashnubbil life in a sitty. It's hily injuyus.

So far yu well, Billy, tel nex time,

MOZIS ADDUMS.

SIXTH LETTER

COCKRUN'S GALRY. THE THEATER. THE SMITHSONIUM. BILL-YUDS. MR. ADDUMS'S FUST VISIT TO THE PRESSYDINT.

DEAR BILLY:

Billy, my sun, lemme giv you a pecs uv advise. Ef uvver you git tanguld with a wummun, nuvver do you taik no ticm to ontie no nots, nor ontangul nuthin; jes tar rite loos, and ef you cant tar loos, pull out yo nife and cut the Gorjun Not and travil. Put yo fingurs in yo ycers and heer nuthen shees got to say. Ef you dont, bi jing! you gone, certin.

I kep on a bodin like a fool at the Mintzpi, the konsequince uv which ware dezastrus in the ixtream. Me and Miz Hanscum—but nuvver you mine a bout I and her. But tware verry plesint thare at the Mintzpi. In during uv them days, cum two marrid ladis thar, the bewtifullist in the wirl. Ethur was anuf to nock a man down with thare lurly boddy and mine, and both together was more'n anuf. In adishin uv them, cum a littil Trungil, sister uv Miss Saludy, and she were one uv them ingajin veriety uv gearl that draws you like a mustud plarstur or a wagun and teem. Cum, furthermo, a littil gal from Indanner, like a hed uv white clovur, she were so far to look apun and so sweet!

I tell you, Billy, we all had fine tiems. Havin plunjd into fashnubbil life, I went on doun in the vawtix and kep on doun, fergitting uv my skeam, fergitting uv everything. Sech is the way in Washintun, whar peepil, stid uv tendin too thar bizniss, goes to spendin uv munny and injoin uv themself like the wild. What with catin and a drinkin and a smokin uv segars, and a goin to Kongis, and to the Patint Offis, the Theater, the Smithsonium, and Cockrun's galry, it ware gloyus. Time floo, and ixpensis wuz hevvy.

This heer Cockrun's galry gits its naim from a white marvel gal, rite start bodily nakid, standin on a velvit stump in the fer eend uv a room filled with paintid pickchers. It's mighty pritty, Billy, mighty pritty; and I reckin a bout the best form-did gal in Emerriky I wisht I cood a seen her drest fur a Hop. and seen her set doun and talk. I jedge sheed a made a impreshin.

A Hop, Billy, air a danse they has every nite in the parlers uv the big tavuns. Oans, a roscul! carrid me the fust tiem to wun at the Mintzpi Hous, and bleevin what he tole me, and he dooin uv the saim, thar we went a hoppin round the room like a cupple uv mainyaks, stid av dansin as we ought to. Nuvver did I heer peepil laf so senst I wer born.

The Smithsonium, whar the Cluk uv the Wether livs, with his insterments to mezure the ar and the wrain an tellin uv a hot day from a cole wun, you goes to heer lecktchurs on vayus subjicks. Lecktchur air a kind uv sermun, without enny trimmins, no tex, no singin uv hims or prars or docksollygis. I heer a man thar lectchur which he had bin to the Noth Pole and staid thar two years. Oans sais he sed the Noth Pole ware a simmun tree full uv peckerwood nesses, but I diddent heer him say so. Then agin, peepil goes to the Smithsonium for no resin at all, excep twuz to nock roun and look at a room full uv potrits uv Injuns. And I ubservd it fer a cuyus fac that the peepil what goes to this bildin in the day time, when thar aint no lecktchurs, is ginerully a yung man and lady, which luvs mitely to be by themself, and the yung lady is alwais verry moddis, warrin uv a vale and turnin uv her hed so you nuvver kin see her fais. And I ubservd the saim uv yung men and ladis, goin in pars and wandrin round in the seller uv the Captul.

At the Theatur thar is fo kind uv plays. Thar's Trajiddy, and Kommedy, and Fars, and Ballay. You've see a littil nigger, when he thot no boddy warnt a notesin uv him, snatch a sweet tater out'n the ashes and run roun the chimbly and goes to gobblin uv it up quick befo sumboddy cums and ketch him. You've see how he blewd and suckd and puft and swet and skrude his feechurs and popt his eye, caus the tater is so hot. Well, that's Trajiddy—that's the way the main man, which ginerilly gits killd, duz, and peepil sais it's verry fine.

You've see a self-cunseetid, nonsensicul po gal jes frum skool. cummin for the fust time to a littil gethrin, a candy pullin or the like uv that. Two or three bows gits to runnin on to her, and you've see how she riggils and twisses and lafs and lafs and lafs at nuthin at all. That's Kommedy, and the main wummun duz izzackly that way, which ameuzis the peepil verry mutch.

As fer Fars, that's a kind uv short Kommedy, a boundin fer the mose part, ef my reckollechshin surves me, in nasness uv idee and speach. Sum uv um is pritty funny tho.

But the Ballay takes um all down. Dingd ef it dont beet my time. Ballay is dansin on the stage, and sich dansin! I'll be blamed ef uvver I see or dreemd uv. I went to the fust wun with Oans, which sed we must git seets neer the stage, rite by the pen whar the fiddlurs and men blowin on the French horn and beetin uv drums—all uv which is called Orkistur—sets. The lady that was goin to doo the best dansin were naimed Seen-yo-een-er Rollar. She were a bewtiful black-har'd Spannish lady, and soon arfter we set doun, and the music had playd and the curtin rolld up, she cum out like nuthin you uvver imajind. Magniffysent, Billy, with a par uv wings to her nakid shoaldurs. Her frock were spangild with dimunds, it were white is a clowd and fine is a fog, and I wisht I may be dernd ef it cum to her knees. I skeersly no what I shell call them things in a lady which I shell call laags in a man, but whatuvver they is, in her cais they was splendid, eakul amost to them thar uv Cockrun's marvel gal, and makin the cole chills run over you to look at um.

Well, Ser, she went a skippin and a hoppin and a pirootin aroun on the flatform uv the stage, like a hummin berd, and pritty soon she cum rite in frunt uv me cleen to the edge uv the stage, facin uv the congegashun, and shot her foot rite smack up to the seelin. Ef you had a stobd a derk thoo and thoo my hart, it coodint uv jumpt no mo than when she dun it. I leetil mo to faintid. Oans he lafft rite out, and the congegashun hoorawd and clapt, and stompt like the fewry. She kep on a dooin uv it, and a fello drest tite is his skin cum out and flung her over his hed and dun I dunno what all, and the peepil hoorawin and a goin on wuss than befo.

I were so shamed I darsent hardly look up, but the ladis and gentilmen blongin to the first famlis uv Washintun hily apruved uv it all. You kin jedge uv yo oan kunclushins in the case what must be the nacher of Washintun sosiety.

In adishin to these heer amewsmints, the men peepil uv Washintun have a way uv a spendin uv thar spar tiem in the day that is verry kuyus. It is a playin uv a gaim by the naim uv the gaim uv billyuds. They takes a tremendus pianner and takes out all the insides—the music fixins—and kivers the hole top uv it with a green cloth, makin a big tabil uv it, with the edges of the tabil turnd up like the edges of a stew pan. At every wun uv the cornders and in the middle uv the two long sides uv the tabil is put a rettykewl, makin uv six rettykewls in all. On the tabil thar is fo balls, too white and too wred. One uv the white balls is got a fly spec on it, which fer the resin they calls it a black ball. The felloes that's a goin to play, taiks in thar hand a whiteoake whip staff without enny thong at all, but havin the eend uv it pintid with a littil pees uv soul lether a bout the sise uv a ten sent pees. These heer whip staffs is called Qs. Each fello taiks his Q, chorks the soul lether on the eend uv it, and perseeds to job the balls at wun nuther and into the rettykewls on the sides and cornders uv the tabil. Over the tabil a passel uv white and black nutmegs is strung on a wier to count the game. A nigger stands by with a pole havin a fiddle bridge stuck to wun eend uv it, to snatch the balls out uv the rettykewls and put um back on the tabil and keep the gaim with the nutmegs. And, wood you bleeve it, Billy? the peepil uv Washintun play at this fool game all day and all nite! You may talk a boute the igronunce uv kuntry foax, but I'll swar they aint to be cumpard with toun peepil.

I shell now tell you uv my ferst vissit to the Pressydint, which happind sum tiem ago, but I has bin ruther techy on the subjic and thot I wouddint tell you nuvver. But I will.

You see in prosekewtin uv my mane desine in cummin heer, I maid cute inkwiris rellatif to my skeam, and cunclewdid from whut I heerd, it were best to go rite too the fountin hed, that is the Pressydint, Mr. Wilyum Cannon himself. I had sum konversashin with Oans on this pint.

 S'e. "Is it a matter uv much impawtense?"
 S'I. "Uv the utmus."

S'e. "Then yo bess way will be to sea the Pressydint privitly. I kin manidge it verry eazily fer you."
S'I. "I shell be a thousun tiems a bleegd to you."
S'e. "Not at all."
So that verry nite we drest up cleen and startid. Stid uv goin up the Avnew, we went down in the dreckshun uv the Captul.
S'I. "You goin rong."
S'e. "No. We inten sean uv the Pressydint privitly, you kno. Uv koas we dont go to the White Hous whar evvry boddy goes, but we gits to see him privitly at the dwellin uv a fren uv his whar he goes uv a nite on speshil bizniss."
We went on doun by Broun's Tavun and the Gnashnul, and I reckin twuz a squar further. Thar we went in a opin passidge and up a par uv steps, and the fust thing I kno we cum to a iun dough.
"Thunderashin!" I sais, "what's this!"
"This ar a iun dough," sais Oans, "to keep the No Nuthins and Plug Uglis from a cummin in heer and a killin uv him."
"Jess so," I sais. "Consoun thar soles! I'd like too sea um try it while I'm heer."
Thar were a roap with a tossil to the eend uv it hangin by the dough which Oans ketcht it and wringd a bell inside. Then a leetil Veneshin blind in the middle uv the dough slatcht opin, a fello looked thoo it and seein it were Oans opined the iun dough and we walkt in. Rite into the mos bewtifull poller, Billy, you uvver sea, full uv splendid fernicher, paintins uv the Possils and Marters, and a lady huggin uv a tollibly nakid baby, a heap mo things, and sum sevril gentilmen a reedin uv newspapurs.
S'I, trimblin, "Whar is he?"
S'e. "In the nex room."
I lookt and thar wuz anuther poller, prittier then the ferst, with a heap mo pictchers, splendid lookinglassis, and enny quantity uv gentilmen settin roun a tabil whar thar were anuther gentilmun doin uv sumthin I coodin sea. Up over the hed uv the gentilmun behine the tabil wer a paintin uv a temendus Tiger, and I notist arfterwuds thar wer a Tiger paintid on the carpit uv both pollers.

Oans seein me lookin at the Tiger sais.

"This hous are the privit rezidints uv the Minister uv Bengall, and that's why hees got the pictcher uv the Tiger, becaws the Tiger ar the emblim uv the Bengall peepil jes like the Egil is the emblim uv the Emerrykin peepil."

"To be sho," sais I, "but," I sais, "aint thar a mighty heap uv seegar smoke here? and I heer a powful rattlin goin on at that ar tabil and I think I distinguisht the soun uv a oath."

"Oh!" he sais, "the Minnister uv Bengall is a fine fello and lets evvry boddy do is they please."

"Rite whar the Pressydint is?"

"Serting, the Pressydint dont keer."

"But," I sais, "who s that littil ballheddid yaller man in the jamp-jackit, standin thar? Pears like hees watir on sumboddy."

S'e. "That's a verry distinguisht man. That's Dred Scot. the Envoy Extrawdinerry and Plennypotencherry from Sain Dominger, that the Spreame Kote made sich a fuss a bout."

S'I. "I think I has heerd the naim befo. He aint white tho, Oans."

S'e. "Sertny not. Hees a Dommynicker man."

"But he wasnt speckild, Billy; he were regler yaller, like enny mlatter."

Oans maid me taik a seegar, and took me to a side bode whar thar wuz evvry sort uv licker set out, and giv me a drink uv prime whiskey, and then we took cheers by the fier and smoakt. I listened good, and I dont think I uvver heerd sich swarrin in the necks room in my life ixcept in ole Swomplanzis room that nite, when the yung Kongismen Joans and Bosin wus thar. I tole you uv it, Billy. Then thar wer a kontinyul rattlin and a rattlin.

The man a settin behine the tabil would say, "Awl reddy?" "Awl set?" and then sech anuther goin on, good*ness!* One fello sais "Hold!" anuther sais "Hold yo hosses." "Dont tern," sais another. "Take them red wuns out'n the pot and put um behine the tray," "Let *them* run to the dews." And they kep a rattlin and a rattlin. A fello sais "Roll," anuther sais "Rip um, dam um."

Then they all shet up, and a minnit arfter cummenst a cussin werse than uvver.

"Bi G—d, I raked him fo and aft." "Took him, dam him." "Well, I fell fer menny a skad." "That's a dam sweet Jack, aint it?" "Yes, a h—ll uv a Jack" "I've bin a buckin aginst the—thing all nite, and d— me ef he aint took me evry tiem." "I tole you so; noboddy but a —— fool woud a kep on when he seen um runnin wun way all the tiem." "Well, I dont want nun uv yo advise," and so on, and so on, and sich a rattlin and a rattlin.

I sais to Oans,

"In the naim uv cents whut's the meenin uv this heer rackit?"

"Oh!" he sais, "that's nuthin but diplomesy."

Which he ixplaind diplomesy to meen the quorlin uv grate men when they tries the destiney uv nashins with keards.

"Well," S'I, "whoos the man behine the tabil?"

"That's Mister Deeler."

"Yes, I heerd um call him Mr. Deeler, but whoos Mr. Deeler?"

"The Minnister from Bengall, uv koas."

"Well, he *hav* a forrin look," I sais.

Then he tole me the naims uv all uv um, but when I assd him to interjuice me to the Pressydint, he tole me to wait tel the diplomesy ware over. I assd him then to pint him out to me, and he pintid at him, but I cooddint see him owin to the crowd, which kep increesin, tho sum went out okashinally. The cussin and the swarrin and the smokin went on at the tabil.

Presintly ole Mr. Dred Scot cum in with a yung persin that sertny ware a nigger, tho Oans swo he wuz a Injun Printz from Centril Emerryky, (enny how he had wooly har,) and Dred Scot he tole um supper ware reddy. Immejitly most uv um quit thar diplomesy and went in a fer room back. Sum remaned at the tabil with Mr. Deeler from Bengall. I wuz a wotchin uv um goin in to supper, when Oans he techt my arm and sais,

"Thar he is; dont let him see you a lookin at him."

And thar he set, Billy, the Cheef Majistrait uv the Yunitid Staits, which I thought his har were gray, but twuz blac, died,

Oans sed, fer an evenin party, a powful, dark cumpleeted man, imposin in apeerunee, a settin in a eheer a reedin uv a paper.

Fergittin uv what Oans tole me, I stard at him like ennything, and he keteht me. When he walled his great big blac eyes at me, Billy, I ware reddy to giv rite up, thar wer sumthin so overpowrin in the idee uv bein lookt at by a Pressydint, I coodn keep my eyes offen him, and, seein what a fool I ware, he got up and cum rite at me. I were goin to run, but Oans hilt me.

Sais he, in the plesint vois uv affability and a smilin at the saim tiem. Sais he,

"Wont you walk in and take supper? You'll find a verry good supper in the neeks room. Walk in."

S'I. "I'm a thousin tiems ableeged but ef you'll please to ixcuse me sir, I aint hongry."

"Well," he sais, "walk in with yo fren and taik a eup uv coffee, a glass uv wine, or you and your fren kin taik sumthin here at the side-bode."

Oans he farly pulled me away. I dident wanter go a tall, the Pressydint he talkt so frenly, and then agin I deside to see him on privit bizniss, you kno, but Oans he sed it ware kuntrary to ettyket to see him on privit bizniss befo we eet.

Well, sir, we went inter suppur, and by the livins! they had thar mighty nigh evry thing that uvver went doun the nake uv man—beef, muttin, vensin, ham, terky, dux (uv a kine they calls canvis bax,) fouls, oshters, homny, pesurves, piekil, vavus kines uv bred, inelewding uv buekwheet eakes and waffuls, selry, plums, ammuns, filbuts, and evrything in the werld to drink, from tee up to the squirtin kine uv wine they eall shampane. The diplomesy men, sum uv hoom lookt like I had seen um befo in Kongiss, was a talkin uv pollytix, eussin and ectin like the devvil, and me and Oans jes wadid rite in and eet and drink the squirtin wine tel we like to bustid. Nuvver did I injoy seeh a meel befo, the memry uv it lingers with me evin yit.

Arfter supper, feelin fine and fred uv nuthin, I walkt up to Mr. Dred Seot, the yaller Dommynieker man, and tole him I wantid to sea the ole man privitly. I ealld the Pressydint the "ole man," jes to show Scot how I warnt no strainger in the plase and felt apun turms uv equolity with enny man.

Scot he sed the ole man ware gone to bed—retide for the nite, and Oans he cummin up about that tiem giv the Envoy Ixstraw-dinnerry from Sain Dominger a quorter, and what astonisht me, he took it, and sed we must "call agin." And we leff without me seein uv the Pressydint in privit a tall. But I ware glad to hav see him enny way, becaws he perduced a favable impreshin upon me. He ware sertny verry amebil and perlite.

Yose constuntly,
MOZIS ADDUMS.

SEVENTH LETTER

MOZIS AND MAYAN. A RESOLUTION. A FIGHT. MOZIS ARRESTED. HORRID TIMES. THINGS CLEAR OFF. SECOND VISSIT TO THE PRESSYDINT.

Dear Billy:

I cum hoam fum a vissitin uv the Pressydint in high sperrits. The squirtin wine had got into my hed, which it felt like a housraisin wus a goin on somewhar, or ruther like the publick mind ware roustid apun a impawtant subjick of genrul intris. Thar apeared to be a goad eel uv ixsitemunt, and I had a inlarged vue, as it twuz fum sum mountiug eminents. Ouns he poked off to one plais or anuther, levin me to entur my bodin hous aloan but puffickly cuntentid and rezined. The fust thing I heard it were little ole Melloo a skratchin on his fiddil and a makin uv prehaps the sicknest and horowblis souns in the wirl. He can't play no fiddil. The neckst thing I dun, I run aginst Mayan in the dark—snatcht her rite up, carrid her in my room. shet the dough, and lockt it, detummined to diskover the reesin she spoke Inglish sumtiems and then agin Irish sumtiems, or dy in the atemp. She ware sollid, Billy, is a wannut stump, wayin, I jedged, a hundud and fotty poun neet, but she warnt nuthin but a shuck boalstur to me, feelin is I did. Mo rover, it ar a noan fac that a man, mo ptickly ef he ar yung, kin toat mo gal, mo ptickly ef she ar yung and pritty, then uv enny uther substunts uv nater, whether uv the anemil, vedjetubble, or minrul kingdum; and I candlely bleeve that eavin a par uv muels kin haul fo to one, by wate, uv gearls to enny uther kine uv truck.

I hadin sean Mayun to speak to her fer I dunno when. So I set her doun on a cheer, lit my lamp. set doun myself, and lockt at her and sed nuthin. I diddent knew what too say. I had dun dun the thing almost befo I knowd it, thout knowin how I cum to do it, and had nearly forgot what I dun it fer, igzackly. She lookt at me mad is fier.

"Is it outin yo centsis ye ar?" she sais.

I shet my mouth hard.

"I do be thinkin its murther ye ar arfther."

I sais not a sillybul.

She jumpt at the dough like litenin, but I ketcht her, took the key out and put it in my pocket. She fit de-prit, but I hilt her, and finely set her back in the cheer agin, while she set thar pail is flour, pantin fer breth, and lookin at me with her black eyes like sheed burn me cleen up. I set puffickly still and diddent bat my eye wunst. Then she giv up. She took to cryin like I don't warnt to see noboddy cry agin. I drord my cheer up and took her han; she thode me off like I'd been a mockersin snaik and cryd mo then uvver. I tried it agin; she thode me off agin feerser then the fust time, and kep on a cryin. I getherd a pipe, filled it with that good Linchbug tobarker, and pretendid to smoak. But I ware skeerd. I ware feard sheed kill herself, she cryd so. I begged her, I sais:

"Mayan, fer the Lord's saik don't cry so. I don't mean you no harm. I'd die ten thousin deths befo I'd hert a har uv yo hed."

But that maid her wuss. So thar we set,—she a cryin and I a trimblin. You may depen I wrepentid what I had dun. I got up and opined the dough, onlockt it, and spred it wide opin. She stopt in a minnit. She got up to go out, still a sobbin, but makin no noise. I put my han on her shoalder verry gently, and sais:

"Pleas don't go, Mayan."

She didin pull mighty hard, so I jes led her back eesy, and set her doun agin, and she commenst a cryin but not like befo—peard like it come mo softer to her. I hitched up my cheer clost to her, tryin to taik her han, but she pulld it away, slowly tho' Arfter while, she lookt up at me, her buteful black eyes full uv teers, and sais mighty sorrerful and wreproachful, she sais:

"Mistur Addums, you ortint to do me soe."

"Thar now, thar now!" I sais, jumpin spang outin my cheer; "thar now! I ketched you. By gravy!" I sais, "that's no

Irish talk, and you aint no Irish nuther. Now you got to up and tell me evvry single bit about yoself. Yu've bin a possummin long anuf, and you shant go a step tel you tell me. You sertny shell not."

She lookt at me like sheed look me throo. Then she smiled a littil bit uv a smile, but her eyes still full of teers, and sais sollum is possybil:

" Then shet the dough."

I shet it, quick.

" Lock it," she sais.

I lockt it. I ware comin back to taik my seat, when she sais in the saim sorrerful vois:

" Hadint you better blow out the lite? Some uv the gentilmen might wanter cum into sea you."

" Well!" thinks I, " this beets the beet." But I blode out the lite and sais nuthin.

Then she made me to go with her to the back winder, whar the moon was a shinin over the houstops, and thar we set doun, and she tole me everything. I shill tell you awl about it sum these dais. Shees a wrispectable girl, Billy, hily ejukatid, and uv good parrintidge—a reel lady, in fac. Her father is a kine uv preecher, which they calls in Iland a Q-rate; gittin monsus po pay, sumthin like a sirkit rider, which he's a gentilman nuvvertheless. She ware a high-sperritid gearl, which rund away becos her father marrid her step-muther and she coodint git along with her. When she cum to this kuntry, she took to talkin like the rest uv the charmber mades, and took to doin uv hous wurk, becos she sed it ware the ferst thing that come to hand, and, arfter tryin it, she liked it becos it kep her helthy and in good sperrits. Her farther have sent her munny to come hoam wrepeetidly, but she wont come, on a count uv her step-muther. She staid in Knew Yawk a ear, then come heer, whur she's bin goin on 2 ears. This ar a meer outlyin uv the fax uv the case, Billy, but it's the plane truth, and nuthin elts. What a pictcher uv the sersiety uv the grate sitty uv Washingtun. A white gearl, a pritty gearl, a reel lady, with fotty times the cents uv the womun that hize her, watin on evvry Tom, Dick, and Harry! It's two bad, two bad intily! and ortent to be so no longer. I ixpec thars menny anuther po gearl jes like Mayan is, and she sais so two.

We had a long, long happy talk thar by the winder. I declar, Billy, I nuvver felt so sosherbil and sattisfide in my life. She seamed to plais so much confidents in me, like I wus her bruther, or kussen, or sumthin. It tetched me to the co. A cloc striked 2 befo we partid, and then I didn want her to go, but she sed she must. I giv her my lamp, she lit it, tole me not to say nuthin to noboddy bout what she had tole me, tole me good nite, and when she got part way up the steps, stopt, and smilin doun at me tole me good nite agin. Oh Billy, Billy, hunny ar wirmwood cumpard to the speach uv wimmin sumtimes. Gudness nose! it doo appear to make a feller's hart melt in his bress.

I didn sleep nun that nite; I didn cavin ondress. I jes laid on the bed thinkin, thinkin, in a sort uv trants, and shood uv hav laid thar fur uvver, ef, a bout the braker day, Mr. Argruff, he hadinter cum in. His face ware gassly and evil beyond amost ennything. He dropt intoo a cheer and bowd his hed upon the tabil and giv a grone—sich a grone! it friz the blud in my verry vanes. Then he looks up, like he diddent no whar he ware, and begins to cuss hisself orful, orful, and call hisself fool, fool, fool, like he wisht he cood tar his hart out and distroy hisself with his own langwidge. I jumpt offin the bed and run to him and begd him to tell me what the matter wus. He give a start saim is ef heed bin shot. Billy, he ware drunk. His breth had that ar green, pizenus odor uv a man which drinks a heep and constunt. He thought he ware in his oan room, and when he foun whar he wuz, and seen me good, he new me, he begins a cryin, and *sich* cryin—Mayan's warnt nuthin to it. It ar a turrabil thing fer to sea a man cry is he dun. It mighty nigh killed me, cos I has a high apinyun uv Mr. Argruff.

When he got over his fit, at least the wust uv it, he let me know all bout it. Betwixt his intruption uv his wremarks with fust a cryin and then a cussin uv himself, I cood barly make out whut he sed, ixcept it twuz this: That ne were in love with a yung lady, which I shant call her name, and had coted her, and she had kickt him, and he goes and gits drunk, and the fust thing he node he had dun gone and seed her farther, and tole him how he loved his dawter and awl about it. Did you uvver heer uv sich a thing, Billy? It ware enuf to make him cuss hisself, and mo too. When he cum to tell about it, I thought heed a gone distracktid with shaim he ware so mad with hisself.

I cumfutted him the bess I cood, which it ware ruther po cumfut, tride to maik him lay down in my bed, but he wooden let me, so I tuk him two his oan room, ondrest him, put him to bed, and left him.

My hart ware hevvy is led, thinkin how the bess pepil in Washingtun seamd to be a flicktid with sum dredful habbet or anuther, and how retchid a life the happist uv um leeds, when I come away frum the hous whar Mr. Argruff bodid. I felt like I wantid to git away frum thar and git hoam whar thar wuz sum quiat and pees, and whar pepil, ef they aint smart, is sertny natchrul and contentid.

When I cum to the Mitzpi Hous, and had eet my breckfuss, Miss Saluda Trungil and her little sister got arfter me, pleggin me most to deth. Fust they tole me my sweetart, Miz Hanscum, (which she nuvver wuz no sweetart uv mine a tall,) had dun rund away with a feller, and gone posably to the devvil. And I diddent keer ef she had. Then thy kept a makin me tell bout my vissit to the Pressydint, and the mo I tole how kinely the Pressydint treatid me and how much I wer pleesed and all, the mo they lafft and lafft, untel I thought nar one uv um had good sense. No wonder they lafft; for ef you bleeve me, Billy, I hadint sean no Pressydint a tall, and the hous which I thought it ware the privit resedints uv the Minnistur uv Bengall wuz, what they call a Forrer Banc. Forrer is sumtimes called Farrow and sumtimes Fareo, and it ar a gaim uv cards, playd out uv a kind uv Seedlitt's Pouder box, and a hole passel uv roun pieces uv ivry; but Forrer as the rightist way to pernounts it. I has sence sean the gaim plaid a sevril number uv times, but kinnot understand it igzackly.

It ware a long tiem befo I cood fairly bleeve that Oans he wood fool me so about the Pressydint, and I don't think now he wood uv hav dun it ef that ar little yaller fiddlin tacky uv a Melloo hadint a put him up to it. I wisht I may be consoun!

5

ef when I foun out he had a prinserpul hand in it, ef I didin hav a good mine to war him out aginst the groun. But, in pint uv size, he aint no mo to me then a huckilberry in a wagun, and I nuvver yit fit a runt and nuvver intens to.

Well, I lef the Mintzpi Hous mad is the verry devvel and distrest in the bargin. It taint so mighty plesint to find peepil keep constunt makin fun uv you and deseevin uv you, which shows the meenniss uv sitty folks, which has sense anuff to tend too thar oan bizniss ef they got enny.

I had dun waitid and waited about that ar skeam uv mine, and spent munny untel it warnt no use in waitin no longer, and I coodin bar to wait a minnit mo. So I goes to my trunc, gits it out, wrops it up keerfully, and goes and shows it to a man apintid to atend to them things. He tole me it warnt wuth a dam. But I sean thoo that. He jes wantid to git me to sell it to him fer nuthin, then he cood maik a everlastin forchin out'n it. So I goes to anuther—thar's hunduds uv um in Washintun, Billy. He sais the saim the fust man sed. So I goes to anuther, and anuther, and anuther, untel I wus broke doun with fateeg and dissypintmint at the meanniss and jellersy uv mankine. One feller did offer to taik and put it thru, ef I'd giv him thurty dollers. I'd a giv ennything, but when I come to igsamine my munny puss I foun I didn hav five dollers in the wirl. This shockt me, cos I knewd I owde fer bode and a good menny uther things. The feller offud to taik whut munny I had, but I tole him no, I ware blees to keep that, and a gread to giv him a writment, a bond, sined with my oan naim. He lafft at me and tole me I wuz a fool. I jes took that thing, wropt it up agin in my hankerchif, went hoam, put it keerfully bac in my trunc, and cum bac and giv that feller the prittiest top-dressin a man uvver had. I masht his pleggid nose flat to his roscully fais, and bungd his eyes that bad that I boun he doant sea fer six munts. He holler'd murder and the patrollers cum and collard me and carrid me befo a majestraint, and I shood uv hav bin ritin to you in jail, ef Oans and Melloo hadint cum and giv bond and scurety I'd behave myself for a year. They let me go, but I didn keer whut becum uv me. I sean the hole wirl ware turned aginst me, and when I cum to ask sum cluks which I had lent munny to, I coodin git a sent, and what to do I didn kno. In the eavnin Oans and Melloo tole me Mr. Argruff ware ded, havin blode his brains out with a pistul, and that that ar fello which I had beet fer callin uv me a fool had challindged me to fite him a dewil, intendin to hav my blud. But it warnt so. Mr. Argruff, disgustid at hisself, had packt his trunc and gone hoam wharuvver that wuz, leavin uv a note advisin uv evvryboddy in Washintun to do the saim, cos he sais the devvil had done took persesshun uv the sitty, havin uv a bill uv sale fer it in his britchis pockit. And as fer that ar feller, I nuvver heerd no mo frum him, sertin.

But my sperrits wuz cleen gone, and whotuvver wood a becum uv me that nite, the Lord only knows, ef it hadinter bin for Mayan, which her reeul naim ain't Mayana bit, but Noahrer Glennun, a verry pritty naim I'm sho, and a better or mo likely and smarter gearl nuvver drord the breth uv life. I coodin stay in the poller uv the Mintzpi Hous, cos all the ladies had got mad with one anuther bout a feller, which I shant call his naime, which wuz a cuttin uv his rustics with all the marrid ladies, and cos anuther man, a membur uv Kongiss, which ware a bodin thar, had bin ketched a kissin anuther man's wife in the passige. Then agin, I ware feerd the man whut kep the tavvun (the Mintzpi) wood ass me for the munny I ode him. And in the hous whar I had my room, things wuz orful bad also, cos I ode munny thar too, and ole Swomplans wuz drunk and rarrin around like thunder and wuss, cos he and anuther Kongissmun had had a quorl. And the Dutchmun and his wife, which had them babis in the wroom abuv me, had goned away; likewise the wrailrode man; and Melloo and Oans, they'd gone off; and things wuz dark and desertid tel I farly thought the nex thing Gabrill wood blo his hon and tiem shood be no mo. And I wure feered to go on the streat, becos the rowdis and Plug-Uglis, which had bin behavin bad all the time sense I set foot in the sitty, had dun broke loose and wuz a shootin and a stabbin and a murdrin and a knockin doun and a draggin out evvrybody that cum along, white or blac, rich or po, or ennything.

But Noahrer she cum to my room and we had anuther nice, long, confedenshul talk, like we had the nite befo. She ar such a good gearl, Billy, and torks sich good Inglis, and, altho she knows I aint so mighty smart, pears to rispeckt and look up to me so. A man kin no mo help trustin his seakrits to a gearl like that than a man kin keep frum warmin hisself by a fier when hees colde. I tole her about my skeam, who I wuz, whar I cum frum, my parrunts, my little plantashun, niggers, hosses, craps, and all. She gimme a heep uv good advics bout trustin too much to peepil, and we all injoyed one nuther's cumpany tell it wuz mighty nigh 2 o'clock in the mornin agin. Nuvver shill I forgit them two nites to the longist day I live, and shill alwais be thankful on acount uv wimnin kind in this worl for the saik of Noahrer, fer ef it hadinter bin fer her, I dunno whethur I shood a bin liftin uv a pen now, Billy. Tell Dellywar Sinker to sell evvry bit uv the con and wheet I kin posbly spar and send me the munny drectly, becos jest is soon is I kin pay off whut I owe, I'm a gointer to maik that gearl a fust rate present, ef sheel taik it, which I'm afeerd she wont, seein how high-sperrited she ar.

Nex day things took a turn. Things peered to clear off, like arfter a long spell uv wrain, when Cat Tail ar a risin tremendus, thretnin to sweep evrything off'n the lo grouns, Noboddy didint dun me fer no munny, and over at the Mintzpi peepil peared to hav maid frens, mighty quick I thought, and afars seamed to be workin well all aroun. Miss Saludy Trungil and her littil sister didn't giv themself no grate greef about a losin uv Mr. Argruff, but went strait ahed, ketchin mo bows, printsply ole men goin to the yung one, and a ball-hedid gentilmun, with gole spectickles, goin for Miss Saludy. They didint plegg me no mo about going to sea the Pressydint at the Forrer Bane, but peared to be pritty mutch wropt up in thar oan afars. The bewtiful littil gearl frum Indanner, she torkt to me sum, and so did them two pritty marrid ladis I tole you uv. I felt heap bettur. Oans, he cum up and apollygized fer foolin uv me at the Forrer Bane. I tole him that senst he had delivud me out'n the strong arms uv the Lor and the Jestis uv the Pees, I had dun forgiv him long ago. Then he sais:

"To maik up fer my bad conduck, I'll taik you to-night to sea the Pressydint in fac."

I tole him he coodin fool me no mo; but he sais:

"Thar's a Levvee to night, and I'll taik you thar, and you can sea not only the Pressydint and Miss Lain, but all the most distinguisht folks in the kuntry."

It ware a long time befo he and the young ladis helpin uv him could perswade me he warnt a joakin, but finely I kunkloodid to go, and my hoops uv my skeam wrevived imeditly. As fer seein uv the Pressydint and Miss Lain, whar evvry boddy wuz, I didint keer so mighty much about it, but I detummind in my oan mine too evale myself uv the okashin to git my projick farly befo the oanly man in the Yuneyun which wuz likely to doo it jestis—vizz: the Pressydint. This heer Miss Lain, Billy, her naim are Miss Haryit Lain, and she ar the gneiss (that's the properist way to spell it, Oans says. In fac, Billy, yuve notist a gradjul impuvemint in my spellin, which are owin to the fack that Oans and Melloo has been kine enuf to devoat a good eel uv atenshun to me on this pint,) she ar the gniess uv the Pressydint.

Well, cum nite, we-all, that is all the ladies at the Mintzpi, Oans and Melloo and me, got reddy. I wantid to taik Mayan, or ruther Noahrer, along, but she said no. Miss Saludy she wantid I and Oans to go long with her and her par in a hac, but Oans sed weed better wolk. Melloo he went with his sweetarts, which is both the littil Trungil and the pritty littil gal frum Indanner, noboddy noes which.

Me and Oans wolked on and wolked on, way up the Avnew, and hax and carridgis rattlin by us and carryin peepil to the Levvee, untel we past Willud's tavun and the Trezry bildin, a powful manshun, fenst in with pillars in the frunt, whar all the munny uv the Guvnurmint ar put in the seller, which I wisht to goodniss I had about a hundud and fo dollus uv it jest about this tiem, and then we wuz clost to the Igzeckutiv Manshin, as the Pressydint's hous ar calld.

Goin along Oans he sais to to me, sais he,

"Mozis, a feller goin to the Levvee fer the ferst tiem are genrully cunsidderubbly imbarist. I faintid the ferst tiem I went thar, and Melloo, bein uv a timmid man, took to his bed for 3 weaks arfter-wuds."

S'I, "Dont ef you plees talk that ar way; you skeer me to deth."

S'e, "Not a tall. I wantid pepar your mine. The way fer a feller to doo, ar jest to act igzactly at his ces, maik himself puffickly at hoam, cos the hous dont blong to the Pressydint, but to the peepil of the Yunitid Staits, which givs it to him, chargin uv him no wrent, and you bein one uv the peepil uv the Yunitid Staits, uv coas it belongs to you much as to ennyboddy elts. You ar jest is good is ennyboddy, and you must act a kordin."

I tole him I ware much ableeged to him fer tellin uv me, ptickly that part about the hous blongin to me, and which tharfo I shood feel intily and puffickly at hoam.

We went on, passin by a heap uv hax and things, goin thoo a iun gate, long a kervd pavemint whar thar wuz mo hax strung out in a lien and mo a comin constunt, untel we got to the White Hous, which ar anuther naim for the Igzeckutiv Manshin. It have a imments big poche in frunt uv it, like the poche uv a Kote Hous, with verry tall pillows, and, kuyus enuf, the hax and carridgis drives right spang into this poche, and one half uv it havin no flo at all but a gravly rode runnin rite thoo it, and the uther half bein paved with rock, and hisetid abuv the groun that you has to go up a few steps to git to it.

Uv the glowry and the splendur, the menny peepil and the bar-armd and barneckt ladies I seen inside, wurds, Billy, kin giv you no idee, not the leest. I ruther think it beets the Forrer Banc and the Ixchain both put together. A white sarvunt, look to me like a Presbyteyun preechur, took our hats and big coats soon's we got in, giv us a brass check fer um like they givs fer your trunc on the wrailrode, and jobbed them in a hole, which they had about a thousun holes made thar for the puppus.

Me and Oans then smoothed our hars and pepard to git interjuist to the Pressydint. I nuvver felt mo nachrul in my life, and wuz rezolootly rezolvd to hav my skeam atentid to that verry nite. In order to git to the Pressydint you has to go throo about twenty diffrent rooms, all openin into one anuther, all uv a diffrint culler, blue and red and green and white, and full uv the most magniffysent fernicher, gilt mostly with gold, and shinin under the gas light tel it farly addles your brane.

The peepil thats goin to be interjuist to the Pressydint forms in a line, two and two, like mustrin, and, arm in arm, goes on frum one room to anuther untel at last they git to the one whar the ole man stands up and shakes hands with evvry boddy. Oans ketcht me by the arm, and we went on and on and on mighty slow, peepil, bar-neckt ladis printsply, befo us, and peepil behind us, and the ferst thing I know, thar wuz the Pressydint—a powful, hevvy-bilt, tall, ole, greyhedid man, with a white crevat, his hed twistid one side, and his eye ruther cockt. Oans ware interjuist ferst, and then a man what stood thar fer the ixpress purpus, grabbed me by the elbow, assed me my naim, I tole him Mozis Addums, and he sais "Mister Mozis Addums, Mister Pressydint; Mister Pressydint, Mister Mozis Addums," and the Pressydint shook me, ruther keerlessly I thought, by the hand, and moved it, kinder pushin me off frum him. But I ware bent apun seein uv him about that thing, so I sais in a verry klectid and oddibul vois, so is to show peepil like I ware used to bein thar, and felt at hoam in my oan hous—I sais, "Kin I sea you a minnit, Mr. Cannun? Jes step this way, ef you pleas."

He jukt his hand away, and begins a shakin hands with sumboddy behine me, pretendin like he diddint heer me, which I knowd he did, cos thar wuz a genrul movemint all around, like sumthin had hapind. I muss say I cunsidud this as bein desididly bad mannurs. He may be a verry grate man, but I and uther peepil hires him by the ear to ten to our bizness, and twuz is littil as he cood do to treet a boddy wrispecktfully.

Enny way I had to leeve him. Lookin roun fer Oans, I coodin sea him, and I sais, "Whar's Oans?" and noboddy anserd, and anuther man ketcht me by the elbo agin, and interjuisis me to Miss Lain, the gneiss uv the ole Pressydint. She ware a splendid lookin lady, drest in black (Oans tole me, arfterwuds. she wuz in monin fer Mr. Lecompting) and havin uv her arms and shoalders bar, and havin, I swar, uv the finist skin I uvver see, white is sattin. I warnt discumbobberated nun, but wremembrin I wuz in my oan hous, sais:

"Good eavin, Miss Haryit, I'm glad to see you lookin so

well this eavnin. Tollibul nise cumpny you got heer this eavnin. Ruther warm fer the timer yeer."

She made me a low curchy, and she said to me :

"I thanky, Sir," she sais, " I'm only tollibul this eavnin," and then she wuz goin to say sumthin mo but wuz took with a fit uv coffin behine her fan, and stopt.

S'I, " You got mighty pritty har, Miss Haryit. You remines me a good eel uv my cussin Betsy Flatback, only she's a dark-skinned gearl, and you aint got no bumps on your forrud, nar a one, is fer is I kin see."

I thought I heern a kine uv tittrin and gigglin a goin on all aroun me, which I reckin I did heer it, and which I has no doubt wuz on account uv po Oans, which jest at that minnit ketcht me and hauled me away, rite throo the croud, which apeard to be a cunsiderbul disturbid, is well is myself, fer his saik. I nuvver did sea sich a fais as po Oans had. Lookt like it ware goin to bust plum opin, it ware so red and so full uv blood. He cum is nigh havin uv a apperplecksy and cunvulshins is enny man I uvver see to miss it. He coodin speak a wird, but hauled me along arfter him, way out uv the crowd, I a thinkin he wuz goin hoam, cos he wuz turribly sick at his *stummuck*. But he carrid me to the eend uv a long passige, whar thar wuz a big glass hous, full uv trees, and the minnit he got thar, he laid down among the tubbs whar the trees wuz plantid in, and rolld over and over like he wuz a gointer die evry secund. I war goin fer a doctur, but he woodin let me. And he made the kuyusist soun, like laffin, and when I sea his fais, it lookt like he ware laffin, but fit to kill hisself with it.

S'I, " Mr. Oans, you laffin, aint you ?"

But his jaw were lockt, and he rolld over and skuffild aroun the tubbs wuss then ever. I knowd he ware in agny, but it sounded so much like laffin I ware bleest to ask him agin :

"But *aint* you laffin, Mr. Oans ?"

It ware a long tiem befo he cood wreply, and when he did, he fetcht breth so hard it ware misry to heer him. He sais :

"Oh! Lord, no. I'm not a laffin. I've got a apperplectic fit. My famly is subjeck to um, and when they has um, noboddy skeersly kin bleeve they aint laffin."

And he laid thar pantin, like a houn arfter a long chaise. I reckin it wuz nigh onto a nour befo he sufishintly rekuverd to git up and go back whar the cumpny wuz. I bresht his clothes, which they wuz full uv dirt whar he had rolld on the flo uv the glass hous, and we went back. But, po feller! he hickupt and gobbled fer breth and his eyes run water so, that evvrybody kep a lookin at me and him saim like we wuz a cupple uv wild anemils, makin it verry onplesant to be thar. So when we cum acrost Miss Saludy Trungil and sum uther folks frum the Mintzpi Hous, which they seamed to hav heerd how bad off Oans he wuz, and he tole Miss Saludy he ware so week he cood barly stand, she offerd him a seet in her carridge, and we giv our chex and got our hats and coats, put um on, and cum back, most uv the uther Mintzpi folks folrin behine us in thar hax. I warnt sorry to leav the seen uv so mutch splendur, becos the cheef objick uv my vissit, that is, seein uv the Pressydint about my skeam, ware knockt on the hed. Comin back Oans ware took so bad agin with his cunvulshins, he ware foast to leen his hed on Miss Saludy's shoalder, and cried and lafft and gobbled thar like a chile. She ware mighty good to him, and took him rite into the poller uv the Mintzpi; and thar I left him and her and Melloo, and neerly all the rest uv um, bein ankshus myself to git over to my wroom, becos, I felt ruther badly.

I hadin hardly got down the steps uv the Mintzpi, befo I heerd the most orful laffin in the wirl in the poller. And thar wuz po Oans, neerly ded with a fitt uv apperplecksy. I doo think sitty folks is the most unfeelin uv humin beans.

Tell um to fix up evrything at hoam, fer I'm a cummin the minnit I pay my dets. I aint goin to stay in this durn plais no longer. Yose truly,

MOZIS ADDUMS.

EIGHTH LETTER.

POOR' MOZIS! NO MUNNY. COMPLEAT FAILURE OF HIS SKEAM. AN IXPLOSHUN. BEDSIDE SEANS. ROW AT MOZIS' WEDDING. BRILLYUNT REALIZASHUN OF HIS SKEAM. THE EEND.

DEAR BILLY:

Billy, why in the wirl diden you cend that ar muny on suner? You mighter saived me a monsus site of trubbil. I tell you I've bin throo the wrubbus sence I last writ, and has sean a wirl uv oneezyness uv mine, and bin nighly ded boddy and sole.

I watid and watid to heer from you. I kep axin the postmaster about yo letter tel he got rite mad with me, and ef he hadenter lived in sech a big, nise, rock hous, and bin pertecktid behine a tremendus winder with only heer an thar a hoal in it—ef it hadenter bin fer this, I and he woulder got inter a fite sertin, becos I ware madder longer him than he ware mad longer me. But nar letter nuvver cum, and I kep on gittin mo miserbler and mo miserbler evvry day, tel I thought I'd giv the gose rite strait up then and thar, and nuvver sea you all and ole Ferginny agin fum tiem tel eturnitty. Winter had dun goned, but spring, whitch putt foth her leaves uv grean an her grass uv grean und her small berds whitch sings in the topps uv the treaz,—Spring fetched no cumfut to po Mozis, owin, I jedgd, mainly to the fact uv the want uv munny, a change uv arr, and turnup sallet which has a fine efec on my livvur. In deede, the joyusnest uv Nacher seamed fer to mawk my stait uv fealins, and the singin uv the birds and the laffin uv the gearls at the Mintzpi Hous, whitch thay wuz boun to keap up with the ceezin, havin uv thar neks and armes barer than uvver—theas heer, apeard speshally to damp my sperrits that bad that no licker nor whisky nor nuthin dum um enny good.

Then agin, Tormentt lookt like it had bust apun the acussid sitty. Knewmerus Kongismens and ofisers uv the Army and uthers had had fites and kep on havin mo uv um, and leckshun tiems a cummin on in the sitty sturd up the biel uv the rowdis tel a inchsreckshun uv niggers ware but a privit wrassil cumpard to um. Evvry nite, *evvry* singal nite and in the day two, rite on the mainist street, sumboddy ware kild, shot, stobd, knockt in the hed, and sumtimes haf a duzzen at a tiem wuz slayd in cole blud.

Oans tole me is menny is 2 hundud wuz throte-cut in 1 day, but this were a speshees uv igzadjurashun whitch subbsurves no good puppus ixcep to friten a man and gits tisum arfter a tiem. He sed he carrid 8 revolters an 2 booy nives on his pussun whenuvver he went out in the streat, and edvised me to doo the saim, but I didden hav nuthin to buy no weepuns with, whitch tellin him, he gose and bize me a bigg gunn loadened with gravvil and tacks, but I got erestid the ferst day I shoaldud itt, and he had to git me outn the hands of the Jestis uv the Pees agin, arfter whitch he got me a hoss pistul, whitch he maid me carry it doun my back in tween my shoalder blaids to keep from bein ubservd, tharby givin me uv a heap uv inkunveenyunts, owing to the thing droppin konstuntly doun into my britches twel I had to tie the butt eend uv it with a twien string, which I hilt in my han all the tiem, and then I felt free to fase a frounin wirl uv all the Plugg Uglis in kreashin.

Thar wuz 1 amewsment that it mite uv hav cunsold me, but fer 1 thing. The Captul yard and the Pressydint's yard bein all grean and the wether bein plezzint uv a evenin, a bigg ban uv mewzisshiners, drest in red cotes like the Brittish, whitch it ar calld the Mreen Ban, yust to cum wunst or twiest a weak and play to hunduds and thousuns uv peepil that flockt to heer um, awl the bewty and the shiverulry uv the sitty bein thar, prantzin and pradin and shoin off thar fine clothes, and little gals in short frocks and hoops runnin up and doun, up and doun, lively as crickits, and evvry thing gay is it possbly cood be. But I didden injoy it nun. Mayan warnt thar, and then agin I ware thinkin uv my skeem, hoam, dets, and a heap uv trubbilsum things.

One eavnin when the Ban ware playin at the Pressydint's grounds, I lookt over the wall and thar, on a littil hill, set a passel uv Injuns, squottid doun on sum rock, smoakin thar pipes, watchin the fashenubbil croud, and thinkin uv thar oan thots. It ware a moanful site to sea, Billy—when a feller wremembud that wunst apun a tiem all the grate sitty uv Washintun yewst to blong to them Injuns' 4-farthers, and now nar one uv um oand anuf lan thar to digg um a graive. Me and them apeard to be like wun anuther fer retchidness. They had loss thar pozesshuns and I had dun loss my hoaps. They wuz fer, fer away fum hoam, and so wuz I. They had no frens, and I had no munny, and I ware goin to say frens nuther, but I wont say that. And thar the bewtyfull musick playd an the pritty ladis and the hansum gentilmen and the happy childun walkt to the soun uv it, and thar wuz me and them po Injuns lookin moanfully on, hevvy-hartid anuf, Billy, and two hevvy—feelin we had no rite to be whar soe mutch injoymint ware goin on and nuthin, nuthin to look forrard to. I cood a cryd thinkin about it, and went away sorrerfull—both fer myself and them po Injuns.

But whut wust a flicktid me and jobbd me doun intoo the verry gulp uv disparr, wer not so mutch the want uv munny an bein away from hoam and all that, but this, Billy. Wun day, that ar ball-heded ole gentilmin whiteh I tole you ware the bo uv Mis Saludy Trungil, and whitch he wars them gole specks I menshind,—wun day, he cum to me, and havin heerd, I nuvver cood tell how, about my skeam, entud into convussashin with me about it. After a good eel uv persuashin I jes canninly tole him all the hole bizniss frum beginnin to een, and eaven took and showd him the thing itself. He keerfully lookt at it, and sed it showd a oncommun amount uv tallent indead, but then he shuk his ball-hed, and makin me go to his apartmint, whar he had a reeul liberry uv books a layin on the flo, and, takin out wun uv the largist volyums, red me the histry uv the subjick, whitch it apears, so fur frum bein aridganul with me, hav ockyupide the mines uv men frum the tiem uv Tuber Kane to the pressint day. Then he ixplained and pruved to me how, in the verry nacher uv things, the skeam ware impossabul and nuvver, *nuvver* cood be dun by noboddy on top of the erth, I diden keer how smart and edjyukatid they wuz. He sholy ar a kine and sentsabul ole gentilmun, and sich I tole him, tho my hart ware fitt to brake at the verry momint. He sed that thousuns uv peepil had cum to Washintun on the saim bizniss pecisely, and he had sean wun uv um, a misubul blind man frum Kaintucky, the day befo. He istablisht to my inti satisfackshun that the mo a man thinks uv this heer kind uv a skeam the wuss it ar fer him, and ef he keaps on he ar certin to go distracktid.

I hilt out is long is I cood, but finely I was bleest to cave in. So, Billy all my vizyuns uv welth and happaniss wuz teetotuly smasht feruvver and feruvver mo. I had nuthin to doo but go back hoam and skratch the saim po man's back whar I had alwais skratched. Thar wuz no help fer it, nun, not the leetlist teenchy bit uv a shadder uv it. It ware a mortil blow. It hert me mo then the tiem you all cut doun the sickamo whar I was up tryin to git a kewn outen his holler, and ef I had'nt bin flung in the lap uv the tree when it falled, I'd a bin killd beyond redempshun. You reckolect I ware ded any way fer haf a day.

All ware certny over now. Mozis, po creetur, had cum to Washintun, maid a fool uv himself, spent all his munny and mo besides, coodin git away, and the hole erth wuz black befo him is the back uv a chimbly. It ware a tiem what tride men's soles. It wuz dubbil and twistid mizry and wo. I hoap and pray you'll nuvver git in no sitch trubbil, ner enny boddy elts, ixcept it wuz the meanist man that uvver lived.

Havin giv up all idee uv my skeam, hatin uv it in fac, I tuc the thing outen my trunc and flinged it outen the winder, but Noahrer, is I arfterwoods foun, getherd it up and saivd it fer hirself. But what she wantid with it I dunno. She did her verry bess to keap my sperrits up, but I ware in the lo grouns uv sorrer and coodint git outen um all I and she cood doo. But I shill alwais luv her fer it. Wimmin, Billy, is the All-heelin Intmint uv the wirl; ef it twarnt fer them we men fokes wood all hav long sence departid this life with ring-wurrum uv the sole, and gone to the land uv shaddus scabby all over our harts, with the 7 ear eetch broke out so bad that no amount uv brimstone doun belo cood uvver cuo us.

Driv to desprashun by cummin out at the little eend uv the

hon with my skeam, I maid the most ankshus inkwiris arfter munny, tryin fer to borry sum uv it. Then, fer the ferst tiem, I cum to a nollidge uv the fac that the hole toun uv Washintun are broke all to peccis, sold in a deed uv truss, bankrup intily. Oans sed he diden hav no munny, sed Melloo diden hav nun, Argruff ware goned away, sed noboddy diden have nun, ixcep it twuz sum men whar makes a livin by lendin uv it at 20 per sent a munth. Its the plain truth, Billy, that thar's men in Washintun which spends thar lives in ruinin the po clucks, lendin um munny at cnawmus intruss, manidjin so that they keep konstunt payin and nuvver do pay out, bullyin uv um too in the most shameful manner. I tell you, cf the haf I heers is the trooth, thees hear men is devvels incarnitt, and one uv um in ptickler is sitch a cole-bluddid, remawsless, diabollikle, infunnil, kon_ foundid ole villin uv a feen that it wood giv me unaloid plezure to menshin his naim and ixpoze him to the papers and to the skorn and indignashun uv mankine. It orter be dun, and sumboddy will do it sum uv these dais, and then I doo hoap and pray that the peepil will jes taik him and all that's like him and bern um to ashes in the publick squarr. It twoodin be no mo then what they desurves, and it wood be a treetin uv me a heap kinder than they has treetid the po clucks for yeers and yeers.

That this sort uv a thing shood be countnuntst in a Cristchun land ar sumthin I kinnot acount fer. The fac that hunduds and hunduds uv abil boddid yung men (sum uv um is old and week tho,) shood let this thing run on without makin enny atemp to put a stop to it, shud let a few rich ole devvels rule um with a wrod uv iun—this fac shose the abjec sperrit, and chickinhartid sort uv men whar lives in toun. Stay at hoam, Billy, whar you kin be free and frade uv nuthin that draws the breth uv life.

But what wuz cuyus and unakountibul to me, ware the sic umunts folrin—that the verry thing which disturbd my mine and which it made me so eegur to borry munny, were the verry thing that nuvver happind to me. I ode fer bode and fer room wrent and washin and uther things to vayus and sundre peepill, I ode um, and, coz yew didden sen the munny, kep on a owin um mo and mo, and nar one uv um dund me. Day arfter day,

I kep on ixpectin uv um to doo it. Thinx I to day I'll ketch it sertin, and whut to say I dunno. But they diden do it—*they nuvver did dun me wunst.* Warnt this straindge? It skeerd me; I diden know what to maik uv it. Tellin Oans about it, it alomd him two. He wremarkd, he sais the like uv it nuvver had happind in Washintun fum the foundashin uv the sitty. Melloo sed sumthin ware wrottin in Dennmok, sertin. But nun uv us kood akount fer it, and yo letter not a cummin, me and the postmarster kep on a quarlin thro the whole in his winder, (I had a gud mine to job a stick in his drottid eye fer him.) So I jes went long, leevin things to Provvydents pritty mutch.

Endurin uv thees miserabul dais, I walkt and walkt and walkt, awl the tiem, to cam my mine ef posbil and git shed uv the site uv so menny peepil whitch the site uv um maid me mad is fier. In fac evvry thing frettid and destrest me. I diden have no pease day nor nite, nowhar, nor with ennyboddy, unlest it wuz Noahrer, whitch I liked her better and more betterer evvry day. I walkt doun to a plase they calls the Knavy Yard, and sean the kannuns and the kannun bawls by the milyuns, and the ships and things, but it dun me no good. I sean um makin uv brass nails thar faster then you kin shell pees, but it jes frettid me. I went to a plais naimd Jawdge toun, a damd-abul horrid plais as uvver wuz bilt upun top the groun, quiut is the graive and derty is a hogg penn, and bein thar maid me feel like I had the pawlzy. I wundud how humins cood live thar. I went to sevril berryin grouns, but the toomstoans urryiatid me.

When uvver I walkt about I carrid my hoss pistul doun my bac, reddy and willin to incownter the Devvil, and all his gang uv rowdis whitch they ar cawld Rams, ef nesseserry, becoz I felt like fitein all the tiem and evvry boddy. But no boddy diden pester me nun ixcep it twuz beggers, whitch jest is sune is I had dun spent every singul solliterry sent I had in kreashun, begun to cum rite arfter me, consoun thar dirty soles! I giv um a pees uv my mine pritty planely, but they diden seam to hav no memry, but kontinyud arfter me evvry day uv the wirl (Mis Saludy sais Oans and Melloo imploid um to doo it, but taint so,) makin uv me so fuyus twuz mutch is I cud doo to keap frum blowin thar miserubbul ole branes outen thar good fer nuthin ole heds uv um, plaig taik um! ding um! My favrit wawk, tho, ware doun to the rivvur at the warf whar the steem botes cum that cum frum ole Ferjinny. I ust to go thar and set and think how happy the day wood be when I cum to go hoam agin, and thar I'd immadjin myself goin back so eesy, ferst on the Orindge rode to Ritchmun, then the Damdvile, then the Sowthside to Fomvil, and frum thar to Kerdsvil, and then rite smac hoam—it seamd like nuthin. But when I kum to wremember I diden hav a sent, then it ware impossybul, intily so, and I mite is well hav bin in the Mune for enny chants thar wuz to git bac. It cumfittid me rite smart tho to set thar and look and look and look twards hoam fer howrs at a tiem, and ef it haden bin fer the Washintun Monyument whitch it seamd to bee konstunt wotchin me, I shood mity nigh hav injoied myself thar.

One mornin I went doun thar rite erly and set way out on the bac part uv a ole steem bote whar noboddy cooden sea me and ass me no questchuns. It ware a powful cool day fer the tiem uv car, makin uv me mo mellunkolly then I uvver had been in awl my life. Peard to me like my tiem had cum, and I diden keer ef it had. I thot about you all, Billy. "Ef I has ar a fren in the wirl," I sais to myself, "it ar Billy Ivvins. But he aint rote to me, and he aint goin to. I wreckin they wreckin I'm ded, and I wisht too grashus I wuz. I'd better be ded than suffer whut I has induode." I fergivd yew all, Billy, but my hart wuz sick, mighty siek. The sun went under the klowds and stade thar, and the wind blowd cold is ice, chillin me to the verry marro. I hoapd it wood freize me ded. But thar I sot, watchin the miserbul rivver that looked so cold and so much uv it, movin up and doun, up and doun, all the tiem, like the bress uv a man with the knewmony or ploorisy fetchin his breth short. So the cold rivvur kep breethen, like it ware in trubbil, had sean a heep uv trubbil and mo wuz a cummin. And then, way, way off yondur, whar hevvin and erth cum together, it lookt dark and shet up, like a hous whar the peepil haden jes gone to cherch and wuz cummin bac bime by, but had gawn away fer good and all. It ware mo then I cood bar, Billy. I drapt my hed, not cryin, but grownin in the growns uv unbarabul agny uv sperrit.

It wuz cleen dark befo I lookt up agin, I diden want to go back to toun. But I diden wanter stay, so I walks mecannykly along, seein and heerin uv nuthin, ropt in my own miserbul fealins. Presintly I heers a loud holrin and seas a brite lite, and, lookin, I seas about too hundud rowdis getherd roun a barl uv tarr, a burnin in a opin plais. One uv um hollers at me, "Hello you dam Plugg, whar you goin?" It sot me on fier at wunst— it ware the verry thing I wantid.

"Cum on!" I sais, "cum on! you villins, I doant keer how menny. You aint a goin to run over me, sertin. Cum on; I be dad shimd ef I doant maik roscul branes cheep in Washintun is oshturs."

Sho nuf, they cum a runnin and holrin like they wuz goin to eet me rite up. But I ware prepard fer um tho. My hosspistul had dun slipt way doun, but I foun the string, and wuz a drawin uv her keerfully up, when they got so clost to me, I gived a hard jirk, and thar ware a ixploshun like sumboddy had blastid the roc uv Gibbrawltur and the Blewridje wide opin, and I node no mo. In the wirds uv the poitry,

  Silunts like a Pole, tis cum,
  The heel the bloze uv soun.

When I cumd two, I wuz a layin in my oan bed in my oan wroom and the wroom ware full uv kumpny. Things all lookt like thees heer insides uv thees heer glass balls they has on parler tabils, and peerd like my centsis wuz outen my hed and a settin on top uv the hed boad uv the bed, a lookin doun at my oan self like I ware sumboddy elts in glass is well is the wrest uv the cumpny. Thar wuz Oans and Melloo, Miss Saludy and her sistur, the luvly littel Indanner gearl, the too bewtiful marrid ladis, and the ole ball-heddid ole gentilmun—all a lookin at me. And Noahrer she set rite at the side uv my bed.

"How pail he is," sais one uv the ladis.

"No wundir," sais Oans, "arfter him a losin ate gallungs uv blud."

"Po feller!" sais the ladis.

"Reckin he'll dy?" sais the littil Trungil.

"Die!" sais Melloo, "not a bit uv it. He's sich a good, simpil mindid anemil, he dont know how to die. You'd hav to giv him a set uv printid instruckshins, with a smal mapp uv the wrout, and evin then, ten chansis to one, he'd git loss. You'd hav to doo is they doo in my country, send a boy with him to show him the way."

"You orter be ashamed to talk that a way," sais littil Indanner.

"Well," he sais, "I will, ef you say so."

"In fac," sais Oans, "he's in grait dainjur."

"Hiesh!" sais the far-har'd marrid lady, "he knows what you talkin' 'bout."

"No he dont," wreplize Oans, "he's lookt jest that a way fer the lass weak, but intily outen his hed."

"Git up frum thar, gearl," sais Miss Saludy, "and lemme smooth his piller."

I see Noahrer's eye flassh fier and the culler cum crimsun to her cheak, but she anserd verry perlitely:

"His piller is nise anuf, Miss, and the Docther sais he musnt be dishtubd, Miss," she sais.

"I doo bleeve the gearl's in luv with Mozis," sais Miss Saludy to one of the ladis.

"Its a spakin fer yeself, ye ar Miss," ansers Noahrer, very sharp.

And then, Billy, evvrything faded away agin.

The nex thing I remembers, it ware nite, and no candil in the wroom, only a feebil lite cummin frum the stoav. Sum boddy ware talkin rite clost to me.

"Poor, poor boy! So fur away frum hoam. No farther ner muther ner bruthers ner sisturs; all aloan heer in this grate sitty, and nun but a servunt gearl to watch over him. The good Lord keep gard over him und pertect him and saiv him."

It ware Noahrer, Billy, and she wuz a cryin. She bent over and kist me. I sais nuthin, but I thot thots. Then she went off a littil ways and kneeld doun by a cheer—she wuz a prayin fer me. I laid rite still, but the teers run like rain, soft teers that cum eesy and plentiful and dun me geod to cry um. I nuvver knowd befo that ennyboddy cood cry them kind uv teers, which wuz so plesint and relievin.

A good menny uther pittyful things happind in this way, Billy, when noboddy didn't bleeve I had enny idee uv whut ware goin on, fer I wuz that weak I didn't keer evin to move, mutch mo speek.

How I cum to be in this deplobul condishin, Oans arfterwuds told me. He's got him a unkil which livs in the sitty, a ole gentilmun uv onhappy sperrits but havin uv a kine warm heart, and this heer unkil wuz a goin hoam the nite I met them rowdis burnin uv the tar barl, and foun me, and had me took hoam, mo ded then alive. I jedge the hoss pistul, which Oans had loadened it to the muzzil with brass tax, went off when I jerkt it—bustid all to flinders, cuttin opin a bigg vane in my hed or nake, and mighty nigh killin uv me. When I ware foun, nuthin ware lef uv the hind part uv my cloaths, sais Oans, but my kote koller and the heels uv my boots, and them had bin on fier, but got put out with my oan blud. His unkil ar uv opinyun that sum uv the rowdis must uv have sufurd is well is myself, thar bein a good eal uv loose flesh layin aroun, which, fer a marikle, nun uv it cum frum me, tho I wuz scorcht horribil.

I wont giv you no mo pticklers tel I see you, which, thank the Lord, will be in a feu dais frum this tiem. Kneethur will I tell you how Noahrer wotcht and nusst me the hole tiem like I had bin her farther, or her bruther, or a littil chile uv her oan, hirin uv anuther gearl her oan self to tend to the hous. Ef she hadent bin pritty, ef she hadint bin smart, I'd a bin bleest to luv her for this. But whut techt me deapist, ware when I got well and she giv me yo letter havin uv the munny in it. Oans hapnin to cum in about that tiem, I told him secritly, fer I diden want Noahrer to put herself to no mo trubbel about me, to tell the lanlod uv the Mintzpie to cum heer I wantid to sea him. So he cum and I handid him the munny, makin no apolligy fer not payin him befo, becos I ware too weak to talk much.

"Why, haow's this," he sais, talkin Yankee, "I guess ye dont owe me nuthin. I calclate yere rite squar up tew the day. You sent me sum munny by that gearl yistiddy."

Noahrer run outen the wroom.

"Well," he sais, "goodby. I got no tiem to chat. Hope you'll be out in a few dais," and away he went like a steem injine is he is.

When the truth cum out, which it diden cum eesy, becos she tride to lay it on sum boddy elts, but it ware boun to cum sooner or later, I found that Noahrer had took the munny her Pa sent her to eum hoam to Ireland on, and had paid my bode, my room wrent, my washin and all with it, spendin uv nigh onto a hundud dollers and a most every eent she had, fer me.

My mine were made up arfter this, ef it hadint bin befo. Soon is I got well enuf to walk bout my wroom pritty strong, I gethurd all my ennergis fer the effut, but the minnit I got to the pint to speek the eole chills and pusprashin broke out and I had to say nuthin. Fo or fiev tiems this aeurd, tel at last I got rite mad with myself fer bein uv sich a cowud, and befo I knowd I sais out loud:

"Noahrer!"

And I sed it so feerse she jumpt up frum whar she wuz a settin sowin, not knowin whut to maik uv it. I ware standin up too. I told her I ment ennything elts but to speek to her harshly, and then ketehin holt uv both her nise plump, littil hands, I sed—I dunno whut I sed—I koted her, trimblin all the tiem tel I coud hardly stand up. She ware bleest to see I ware in erniss, and then she eummenst a trimblin too. Her euller cum and went like fier tryin to ketch—she hung back like a gate with a bad fall—but when she cum, I tell you she cum. That gate slatcht too like it ware nuvver goin to be opin'd no mo fervvver. I must uv hav kist her a thousing uv tiems.

Billy, thar's barm in Gilyud, Billy—thar's a fezeeshun thar, surtin. The doektur frum that deestric hav bin practisin on me fer mo'n a week, and I'm a mendin wrappidly. Git yo Ma and cussin Fanne to go over to my hous and maik the folks cleen up is eleen is eleen kin be. I and Noahrer am a eummin shortly. I forgivs myself fer her saik fer eummin heer to Washintun with my pleggid skeem, but I shell be eonsoundid gladd to git back to ole Buckingame and breeth the ar rite fresh frum Willisis mountin wunst mo.

We wuz marrid a few dais ago, marrid in cherch, not by no Cathlic but by a reglur Baptiss, Noahrer sayin she'd do ennything to plees me, and as fer wrelidgin, she'd alwais bin a Protestunt, altho' she went to the Cathlic cherch. A lardge cumpny uv ladis and jentilmen frum the Mintzpi cum to atend the serremony, but Oans, which I had ptickly countid apun him, ickskewsed himself on acount of bizniss, he bein uv a cluck, you know. The marridje wuz a goin on very nise, altho' I ware rite smartly skeered and week in the knees, when I heers a turbul fuss behine me, and the nex thing sumboddy had dun collard me. Turnin roun, I seen a big ole gentilmun, mighty red in the fais, shakin me by the collar, shakin a gole-heddid kain in my nose, and holrin with a most a powful vois:

"I ferbid the serremony! I ferbid it. He shell not marry my dawter. You villin," he sais to me, "I've cawt you. I'll teech you, you scoundrul, to run away with a gentlemun's dawter. Take that, you roscul!" and he bungd me on the nose with the gole hed uv his kain.

The ladis screemed feerful, and little ole Melloo hollerd out. "it's a mistaik, a mistaik, this aint yo dawter, sir." But I knowd he ware Noahrer's farther, which had crost the sea arfter her, but I didn't keer whose farther he wuz, he shoodint hit me: so I drord off, and I ware is mad is the devvil, and spanged him rite in the middle uv the farrud and laid him cole. Nurver wuz thar sich a fuss uv screemin and holrin—holrin fer the pleece, which they didint cum a tall.

Noahrer run to her farther, whar he wuz a layin flat uv his back on the flo, to atend to him, but she hadint farly techt him befo she bounct up with her fais full uv the most intents disgustt. Twarnt no farther uv hern, twarnt no farther uv noboddy, it ware Oans—a consoundid villin uv a roscul! which had gone and dress up in ole Kongismun Swomplans' cloathes, buttnin up a pillar in his breeches fer fatt, borryin his goleheddid kain, and a paintin uv his fais wred to maik out he ware mad, and cummin playin that fool trick on me and Noahrer. I wer feerd I had kilt him, but he cum to his centsis arfter a while, and wuz well anuf to be at the party they give us that night at the Mintzpi, tho' he had a bump on his farrud which it maid him look like a yung eunuchorn, Miss Saludy sed.

His horn in his farrud, and my bunged nose, made um all laff mightly, and we injoyed the evenin perdidjus. Noahrer wuz alowd by all but the ladies to be the prittiest and smartist lady thar, the gentilmen all falin in love with her, which maid me feal prowd as I dunno whut. Ole Swomplans swo he wuz goin to kill me fer my widder, but he ware jest a joakin.

After Oans wuz carrid outen the cherch the marridje serrymony perseedid nisely to the verry eend—we wuz made tite and fast in the wholly bons uv matrimunny whitch it wrejoyst my heart ixseedingly. When the cumpny all got out and had dun got in thar hax and Noahrer in hern, and I jest about to follow her, Melloo ketcht me by the arm and took me one side, sayin:

"Lemme congratulate you."

"Sertny," I sais, "jest is much is you please."

"I dont mean about your marridje, but your skeem," he sais.

"S'I, "Drot the skeem! I nuvver want to heer it menshind."

"Whut!" he sais, "not arfter so brillyunt a reulizashin uv it?"

I tole him I did'n understand him—no mo I didnt.

S'e, "Hav you lookt at your wife keerfully?"

"Well," I sais, "not ptickly as yit."

"I mean her fais," he sais.

"Sertny," I sais, "I kist her wunst."

"Did you notice ennything pecuelyer about her fais?" he sais.

S'I, "Nuthin, ixcept it twuz mighty pritty and good."

"Well," he sais, "unlest she diffurs verry grately frum enny woman I uvver saw, or uvver herd uv, you will, if you igzamine keerfully, find sumwhar between the nose and chinn a importunt apperchur."

"A apperchur!" I sais.

"Yes," he sais, "a openin."

"Her mouth!" I ixclaims.

"Igzackly," sais he, "and thar in lies the compleat foolfillmunt ur re skeem."

S'I. " Goodness nose! whut do you mean?"

Sais he, "Tharin, that is, in that thar apperchur or openin, or mouth, and in that thar openin aloan uv all places in this werld, you will find PERPETCHUL MOSHUN!"

In haist tel we meat,

Yo ole frend,

MOZIS ADDUMS.

www.ingramcontent.com/pod-product-compliance
Lightning Source LLC
Chambersburg PA
CBHW020302090426
42735CB00009B/1184